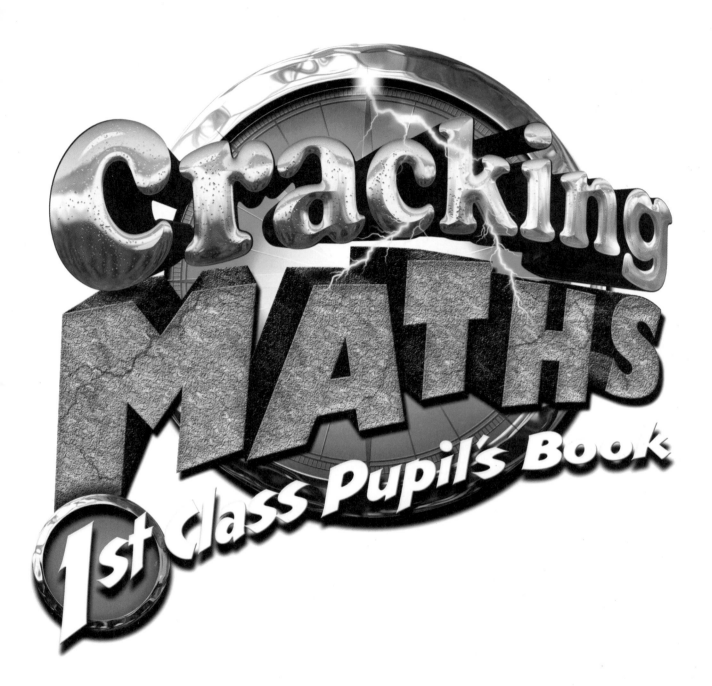

Cracking MATHS

1st Class Pupil's Book

**Majella O'Connor, Aishling Doyle,
Joan Gilligan, Carmel Kelly, Catherine Knight**

g GILL EDUCATION

Gill Education
Hume Avenue
Park West
Dublin 12
www.gilleducation.ie

Gill Education is an imprint of M.H. Gill & Co.

ISBN: 978 07171 54197

© Majella O'Connor, Aishling Doyle, Joan Gilligan, Carmel Kelly, Catherine Knight 2014

Design: Outburst Design and Richard Jervis
Internal illustrations: Derry Dillon
Technical drawings: MPS Limited
Cover illustration: www.designbos.ie
Consultant editor in mathematics curriculum and pedagogy: Betty Stoutt
Mathematics consultant: Oliver Hyde

The paper used in this book comes from the wood pulp of sustainably managed forests.

For permission to reproduce photographs, the authors and publisher gratefully acknowledge the following:

© Alamy: 46, 119 (beans), 119 (sweets), 143 (hula hoop, stickers), 154 (sugar, potatoes, flour), 155 (potatoes, flour, carrots); iStock: 121L; © Shutterstock: 65, 93, 95, 96, 97, 99, 100, 101, 119, 121C, 121R, 125, 129, 142, 143, 144, 145, 146, 147, 151, 154, 155.

The authors and publisher have made every effort to trace all copyright holders, but if any has been inadvertently overlooked we would be pleased to make the necessary arrangement at the first opportunity.

Contents

1. Match the number to the set:

4

1

7

4

2

8

5

9

10

3

6

Curriculum Objective:
To revise concepts that were explored in Senior Infants.

1

1. **Match:**

three

one

five

two

ten

seven

nine

six

four

eight

2. **Add:**

1	2	3	4	5	6	7	8	9	10

3 + 6 = ☐   2 + 5 = ☐

4 + 4 = ☐   7 + 1 = ☐

5 + 3 = ☐   8 + 2 = ☐

3 + 2 = ☐   6 + 0 = ☐

Partition the set.
5 = 3 + 2

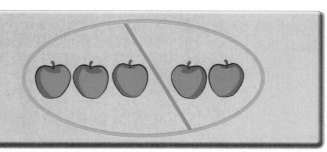

Count and use your pencil to partition the sets:

1. 8 = 4 + _____

2. 7 = 5 + _____

3. 10 = 4 + _____

4. 5 = 1 + _____

5. 6 = 3 + _____

6. 9 = 5 + _____

Add

| 1 | 2 | 3 | 4 | 5 | 6 | 7 | 8 | 9 | 10 |

1.

2 + 5 = ☐   3 + 1 = ☐

3 + 1 = ☐   2 + 2 = ☐

5 + 4 = ☐   7 + 2 = ☐

1 + 6 = ☐   1 + 9 = ☐

9 + 1 = ☐   7 + 3 = ☐

3 + 7 = ☐   1 + 1 = ☐

2.

4 + 3 = ☐   8 + 1 = ☐

2 + 8 = ☐   10 + 0 = ☐

1 + 4 = ☐   6 + 2 = ☐

5 + 3 = ☐   5 + 0 = ☐

3 + 3 = ☐   4 + 2 = ☐

4 + 4 = ☐   3 + 2 = ☐

5 + 5 = ☐   7 + 0 = ☐

Add

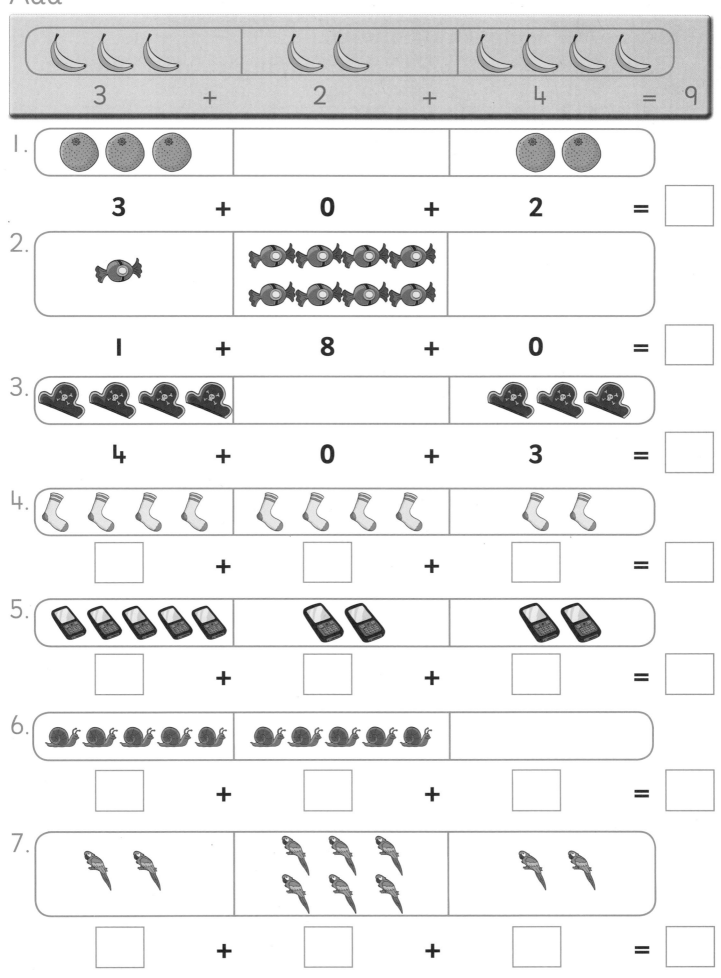

3   +   2   +   4   =   9

1.   3   +   0   +   2   =

2.   1   +   8   +   0   =

3.   4   +   0   +   3   =

4.   ☐   +   ☐   +   ☐   =

5.   ☐   +   ☐   +   ☐   =

6.   ☐   +   ☐   +   ☐   =

7.   ☐   +   ☐   +   ☐   =

2-D Shapes

1. Match the name to its shape.

square	triangle	rectangle	circle

Colour the square red.
Colour the circle blue.

Colour the rectangle orange.
Colour the triangle green.

More Adding!

1	2	3	4	5	6	7	8	9	10

2.

```
    4        5        9        2        5        8
  + 2      + 0      + 1      + 7      + 3      + 2
  ___      ___      ___      ___      ___      ___
```

3.

```
    3        4        7        2        2        6
    1        3        1        4        2        0
  + 2      + 1      + 1      + 3      + 5      + 2
  ___      ___      ___      ___      ___      ___
```

4. Add and colour.

7	blue
8	yellow
9	green
10	red

3 + 4 =

5 + 5 =

8 + 0 =

6 + 3 =

4 + 4 =

4 + 5 =

2. Addition 1

What Makes 10?

$4 + 6 = 10$

| ● | ● | ● | ● | ● |
| ● | ● | ● | ● | ● |

💡 Use your 10 frame and counters to help you.

1. **Use your 10 frame to help you with these.**

$4 + \boxed{6} = 10$ $5 + \boxed{} = 10$ $3 + \boxed{} = 10$

$1 + \boxed{} = 10$ $7 + \boxed{} = 10$ $9 + \boxed{} = 10$

$2 + \boxed{} = 10$ $0 + \boxed{} = 10$ $6 + \boxed{} = 10$

$8 + \boxed{} = 10$ $10 + \boxed{} = 10$ $2 + 3 + \boxed{} = 10$

2. $\boxed{5} + 5 = 10$ $\boxed{} + 3 = 10$ $\boxed{} + 9 = 10$

$\boxed{} + 7 = 10$ $\boxed{} + 2 = 10$ $\boxed{} + 0 = 10$

$\boxed{} + 4 = 10$ $\boxed{} + 1 = 10$ $\boxed{} + 6 = 10$

$\boxed{} + 8 = 10$ $\boxed{} + 10 = 10$ $\boxed{} + 5 + 2 = 10$

3. **Colour 2 balloons that make 10 in each group:**

Strand: Number
Curriculum Objectives:
Develop an understanding of addition by combining or partitioning sets, use concrete materials 0–20;
explore, develop and apply the commutative, associative and zero properties of addition;
develop and/or recall mental strategies for addition facts within 20;
construct number sentences and number stories;
solve problems involving addition within 20;
add numbers without and with renaming within 99;
explore and discuss repeated addition and group counting.

When you add zero the number stays the same.

| 3 | + | 0 | = | 3 |

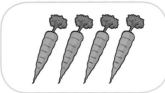  

| 4 | + | 0 | = | 4 |

| 0 | + | 3 | = | 3 |

1. 4 + 0 = ☐   2 + 0 = ☐   6 + 0 = ☐

    8 + 0 = ☐   5 + 0 = ☐   3 + 0 = ☐

    1 + 0 = ☐   7 + 0 = ☐   9 + 0 = ☐

2. 0 + 1 = ☐   0 + 8 = ☐   0 + 4 = ☐

    0 + 9 = ☐   0 + 3 = ☐   0 + 6 = ☐

    0 + 2 = ☐   0 + 7 = ☐   0 + 5 = ☐

3.
3	5	4	6	7	0	0	0	0	0
+0	+0	+0	+0	+0	+2	+8	+5	+9	+0
☐	☐	☐	☐	☐	☐	☐	☐	☐	☐

Problem Solving

There are 3 black rabbits.
There are 4 white rabbits.
How many rabbits are there in all?

3 + 4 = 7 rabbits

1	2	3	4	5	6	7	8	9	10

1.

There are 4 red coats.
There are 5 blue coats.
How many coats are there
in all?

4 + 5 = 9 coats

2.

There are 2 green apples in
the bowl.
There are also 6 red apples.
How many apples are there
altogether?

☐ + ☐ = ☐ apples

3.

There are 7 black dogs.
There are 3 white dogs.
How many dogs are there
in all?

☐ + ☐ = ☐ dogs

4.

There are 8 cats in the
garden.
There are 2 more in a basket.
How many cats altogether?

☐ + ☐ = ☐ cats

5.

2 frogs are in the water.
4 frogs are jumping.
3 frogs are eating flies.
How many frogs in all?

☐ + ☐ + ☐ = ☐ frogs

6.

4 birds are singing.
1 bird is in the nest.
5 birds are flying.
How many birds altogether?

☐ + ☐ + ☐ = ☐ birds

Addition

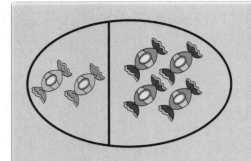 =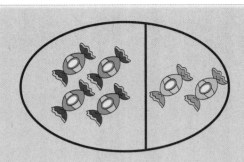

$2 + 4 = 6$ **and** $4 + 2 = 6$

so $\quad 2 + 4 \qquad\qquad = \qquad\qquad 4 + 2$

When two numbers are the same, the answer is the same.
It doesn't matter which way you turn the sum.
It doesn't matter which number comes first.

 =  $\qquad$  =

$3 + 2 = 2 + \boxed{3}$ $\qquad\qquad$ $4 + 1 = 1 + \boxed{4}$

1. $\quad 5 + 2 = 2 + \boxed{} \qquad 5 + 4 = 4 + \boxed{} \qquad 1 + 8 = 8 + \boxed{}$

$\quad 7 + 3 = 3 + \boxed{} \qquad 4 + 3 = 3 + \boxed{} \qquad 2 + 7 = 7 + \boxed{}$

$\quad 3 + 5 = 5 + \boxed{} \qquad 6 + 2 = 2 + \boxed{} \qquad 4 + 6 = 6 + \boxed{}$

2. $\quad 6 + 3 = \boxed{} + 6 \qquad 8 + 2 = \boxed{} + 8 \qquad 4 + 5 = \boxed{} + 4$

$\quad 3 + 7 = \boxed{} + 3 \qquad 9 + 1 = \boxed{} + 9 \qquad 2 + 6 = \boxed{} + 2$

$\quad 7 + 2 = \boxed{} + 7 \qquad 8 + 1 = \boxed{} + 8 \qquad 0 + 5 = \boxed{} + 5$

3. **Draw a picture to show 2 + 3 = 3 + 2**

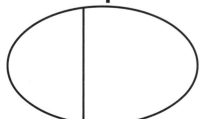 =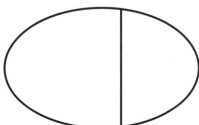

3. Counting and Numeration 1

Eleven

How many?

11   **eleven dolphins**

1. **Colour 1 square on the 10 frame for every dolphin.**

2. **Trace over the numeral 11.**

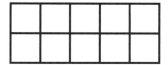 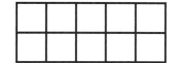

3. **Draw 11 fish** 	4. **Draw 11 balloons**

5. eleven   eleven   eleven

Strand: Number
Curriculum Objectives:
Count the number of objects in a set;

read, write and order numerals, 0–99;
estimate the number of objects in a set 0–20.

Eleven

What makes 11?

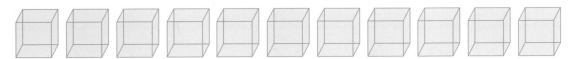

$$6 + 5 = 11$$

Here are 11 cubes and 2 plates.

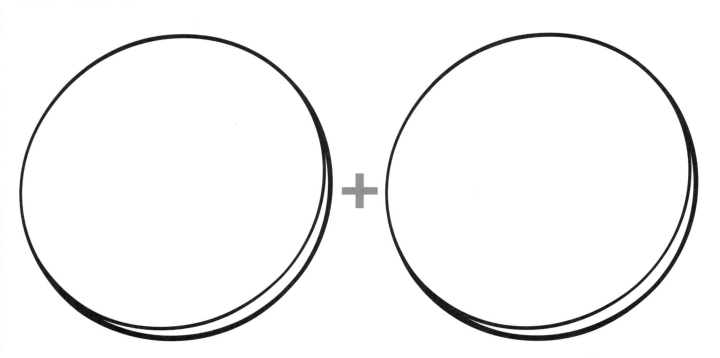

1. **How many ways can you make 11?**

☐ + ☐ = 11			☐ + ☐ = 11		
☐ + ☐ = 11			☐ + ☐ = 11		
☐ + ☐ = 11			☐ + ☐ = 11		
☐ + ☐ = 11			☐ + ☐ = 11		
☐ + ☐ = 11			☐ + ☐ = 11		
☐ + ☐ = 11			☐ + ☐ = 11		

Twelve

How many?

12   **twelve koalas**

1. **Colour 1 square on the 10 frame for every koala.**

2. **Trace over the numeral 12.**

3. **Draw 12 nuts**	4. **Draw 12 leaves**

5. twelve   twelve   twelve

Twelve

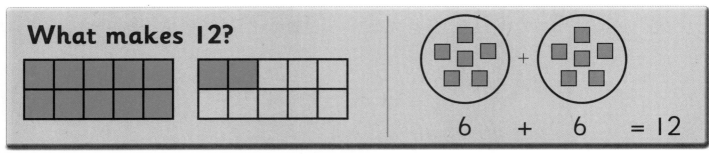

What makes 12?

6 + 6 = 12

Here are 12 cubes and 2 plates.

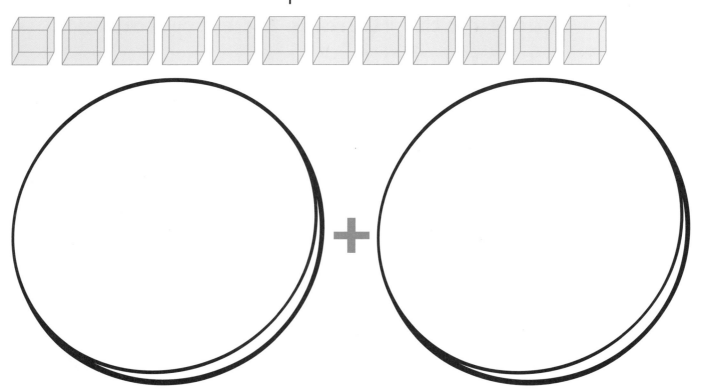

1. **How many ways can you make 12?**

☐ + ☐ = 12			☐ + ☐ = 12		
☐ + ☐ = 12			☐ + ☐ = 12		
☐ + ☐ = 12			☐ + ☐ = 12		
☐ + ☐ = 12			☐ + ☐ = 12		
☐ + ☐ = 12			☐ + ☐ = 12		
☐ + ☐ = 12			☐ + ☐ = 12		
☐ + ☐ = 12					

Thirteen

How many?

13   **thirteen kangaroos**

1. **Colour 1 square on the 10 frame for every kangaroo.**

2. **Trace over the numeral 13.**

3. **Draw 13 balls**	4. **Draw 13 buns**

5. thirteen thirteen thirteen

Thirteen

What makes 13?

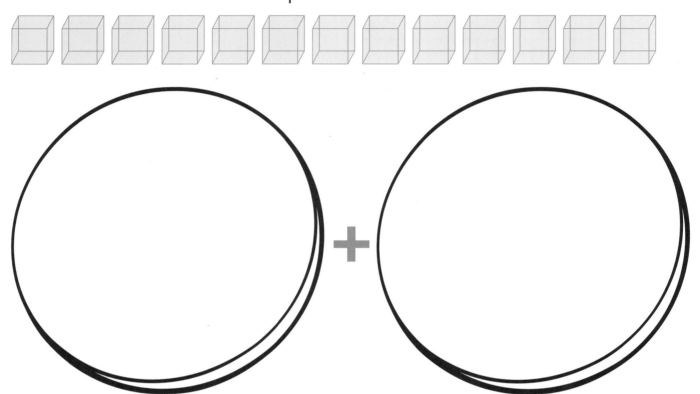

6 + 7 = 13

Here are 13 cubes and 2 plates.

1. **How many ways can you make 13?**

☐ + ☐ = 13		☐ + ☐ = 13		
☐ + ☐ = 13		☐ + ☐ = 13		
☐ + ☐ = 13		☐ + ☐ = 13		
☐ + ☐ = 13		☐ + ☐ = 13		
☐ + ☐ = 13		☐ + ☐ = 13		
☐ + ☐ = 13		☐ + ☐ = 13		
☐ + ☐ = 13		☐ + ☐ = 13		

4. Addition 2

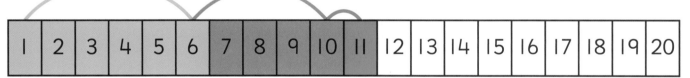

| 1 | 2 | 3 | 4 | 5 | 6 | 7 | 8 | 9 | 10 | 11 | 12 | 13 | 14 | 15 | 16 | 17 | 18 | 19 | 20 |

$6 + 5 = \boxed{11}$

1. Count on, using the number strip.

$7 + 4 = \boxed{}$ $5 + 6 = \boxed{}$ $10 + 1 = \boxed{}$ $8 + 4 = \boxed{}$

$6 + 6 = \boxed{}$ $11 + 0 = \boxed{}$ $11 + 1 = \boxed{}$ $9 + 3 = \boxed{}$

$8 + 3 = \boxed{}$ $4 + 7 = \boxed{}$ $7 + 5 = \boxed{}$ $9 + 2 = \boxed{}$

2.

7	8	6	5	11	10	12	9	6	4
+4	+3	+6	+7	+1	+2	+0	+2	+5	+8

| 1 | 2 | 3 | 4 | 5 | 6 | 7 | 8 | 9 | 10 | 11 | 12 | 13 | 14 | 15 | 16 | 17 | 18 | 19 | 20 |

$6 + 4 + 1 = \boxed{}$

3. Count on, using the number strip.

$5 + 5 + 1 = \boxed{}$ $9 + 1 + 2 = \boxed{}$ $7 + 3 + 2 = \boxed{}$

$5 + 5 + 2 = \boxed{}$ $4 + 2 + 5 = \boxed{}$ $6 + 4 + 2 = \boxed{}$

$4 + 6 + 1 = \boxed{}$ $8 + 2 + 2 = \boxed{}$ $2 + 3 + 6 = \boxed{}$

$6 + 4 + 1 = \boxed{}$ $4 + 6 + 2 = \boxed{}$ $8 + 2 + 1 = \boxed{}$

Strand: Number
Curriculum Objectives:
Develop an understanding of addition by combining or partitioning sets, use concrete materials 0–20;
explore, develop and apply the commutative and zero properties of addition;
develop and recall mental strategies for addition facts within 20;
construct number sentences and number stories;
solve problems involving addition within 20;
add numbers without renaming within 99.

Count On

6 + [?] = 9

Start at 6 and count the steps to get to 9.

It takes 3 steps, so 6 + 3 = 9.

| 1 | 2 | 3 | 4 | 5 | 6 | 7 | 8 | 9 | 10 | 11 | 12 |

1. 7 + [ ] = 11   6 + [ ] = 11   10 + [ ] = 11

    9 + [ ] = 11   5 + [ ] = 12   10 + [ ] = 12

    8 + [ ] = 12   5 + [ ] = 11   1 + [ ] = 11

---

2.   7   6   6   7   8   8   5   10
    +[ ]   +[ ]   +[ ]   +[ ]   +[ ]   +[ ]   +[ ]   +[ ]
    ____   ____   ____   ____   ____   ____   ____   ____
     11   12   11   12   11   12   11   12

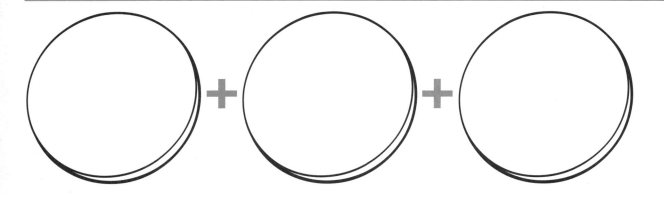

3. 3+ 6 + [ ] =11 | 4+ 4 + [ ] =12 | 6 + 2 + [ ] =11

   9+ 1 + [ ] =12 | 10+ 2 + [ ] =12 | 5 + 1 + [ ] =12

   4+[ ] + 6 =12 | 5+[ ] + 5 =11 | 7 + [ ] + 3 =12

   8+[ ] + 2 =11 | 9+[ ] + 1 =12 | 10 + [ ] + 1 =11

Add

1	2	3	4	5	6	7	8	9	10	11	12	13

1. **Circle the sums that equal the number under the apple.**

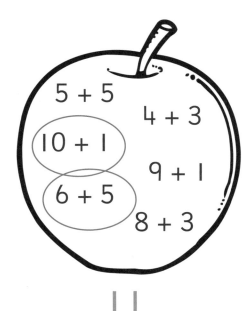

5 + 5
4 + 3
10 + 1
9 + 1
6 + 5
8 + 3

11

6 + 6
7 + 3
10 + 2
8 + 4
4 + 7
11 + 1

12

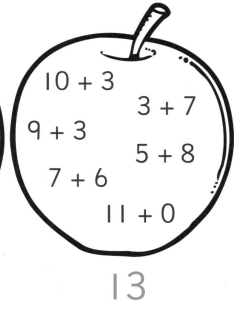

10 + 3
3 + 7
9 + 3
5 + 8
7 + 6
11 + 0

13

1	2	3	4	5	6	7	8	9	10	11	12	13

2.　4 + 7 = ☐ 11　　8 + 4 = ☐　　11 + 2 = ☐

　　8 + 5 = ☐　　6 + 6 = ☐　　9 + 4 = ☐

　　10 + 1 = ☐　　0 + 13 = ☐　　12 + 1 = ☐

　　9 + 3 = ☐　　5 + 6 = ☐　　8 + 3 = ☐

3.　7　　8　　9　　6　　11　　5　　12　　2　　4　　3
　 + 5　 + 4　 + 3　 + 7　 + 2　 + 8　 + 0　 + 9　 + 7　 +10
　 ☐　　☐　　☐　　☐　　☐　　☐　　☐　　☐　　☐　　☐

4.　10 + 1 + 1 = ☐　　9 + 1 + 2 = ☐　　8 + 3 + 2 = ☐

　　9 + 4 + 0 = ☐　　6 + 2 + 3 = ☐　　7 + 2 + 2 = ☐

Fourteen

How many?
14

fourteen dogs

1. **Colour 1 square on the 10 frame for every dog.**

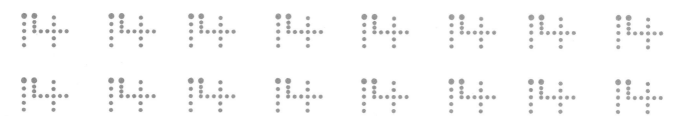

2. **Trace over the numeral 14.**

14   14   14   14   14   14   14   14

14   14   14   14   14   14   14   14

3. **Draw 14 hats**	4. **Draw 14 circles**

5. fourteen fourteen fourteen

Strand: Number
Curriculum Objectives:
Count the number of objects in a set;
read, write and order numerals 0–99;
estimate the number of objects in a set 0–20.

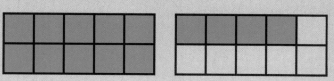

What makes 14?

fourteen

Here are 14 cubes and 2 plates.

$+$

1. **How many ways can you make 14?**

☐ + ☐ = 14 ☐ + ☐ = 14

☐ + ☐ = 14 ☐ + ☐ = 14

☐ + ☐ = 14 ☐ + ☐ = 14

☐ + ☐ = 14 ☐ + ☐ = 14

☐ + ☐ = 14 ☐ + ☐ = 14

☐ + ☐ = 14 ☐ + ☐ = 14

☐ + ☐ = 14 ☐ + ☐ = 14

☐ + ☐ = 14

Fifteen

How many?

15   fifteen robins

1. Colour 1 square on the 10 frame for every robin.

2. Trace over the numeral 15.

15 15 15 15 15 15 15 15

15 15 15 15 15 15 15 15

3. Draw 15 buttons 	4. Draw 15 squares

5. fifteen   fifteen   fifteen

What makes 15?

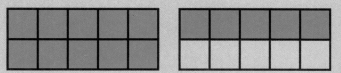

fifteen

Here are 15 cubes and 2 plates.

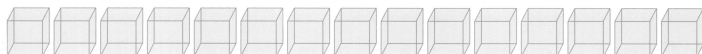

1. **How many ways can you make 15?**

☐ + ☐ = 15			☐ + ☐ = 15		
☐ + ☐ = 15			☐ + ☐ = 15		
☐ + ☐ = 15			☐ + ☐ = 15		
☐ + ☐ = 15			☐ + ☐ = 15		
☐ + ☐ = 15			☐ + ☐ = 15		
☐ + ☐ = 15			☐ + ☐ = 15		
☐ + ☐ = 15			☐ + ☐ = 15		
☐ + ☐ = 15			☐ + ☐ = 15		

Sixteen

How many?

16   **sixteen owls**

1. **Colour 1 square on the 10 frame for every owl.**

2. **Trace over the numeral 16.**

3. **Draw 16 jelly beans**	4. **Draw 16 oranges**

5. sixteen   sixteen   sixteen

What makes 16?

sixteen

Here are 16 cubes and 2 plates.

1. **How many ways can you make 16?**

☐ + ☐ = 16   ☐ + ☐ = 16

☐ + ☐ = 16   ☐ + ☐ = 16

☐ + ☐ = 16   ☐ + ☐ = 16

☐ + ☐ = 16   ☐ + ☐ = 16

☐ + ☐ = 16   ☐ + ☐ = 16

☐ + ☐ = 16   ☐ + ☐ = 16

☐ + ☐ = 16   ☐ + ☐ = 16

☐ + ☐ = 16   ☐ + ☐ = 16

☐ + ☐ = 16

6. Addition 3

| 1 | 2 | 3 | 4 | 5 | 6 | 7 | 8 | 9 | 10 | 11 | 12 | 13 | 14 | 15 | 16 | 17 | 18 | 19 | 20 |

$$6 + 8 = \boxed{14}$$

1. **Count on, using the number strip.**

$7 + 7 = \boxed{}$ $5 + 10 = \boxed{}$ $13 + 1 = \boxed{}$ $12 + 3 = \boxed{}$

$9 + 5 = \boxed{}$ $12 + 2 = \boxed{}$ $11 + 3 = \boxed{}$ $10 + 4 = \boxed{}$

$8 + 6 = \boxed{}$ $4 + 11 = \boxed{}$ $13 + 2 = \boxed{}$ $8 + 7 = \boxed{}$

2.

7	10	8	12	9	7	11	13	14	5
+8	+5	+6	+2	+6	+8	+4	+1	+1	+9
$\boxed{}$	$\boxed{}$	$\boxed{}$	$\boxed{}$	$\boxed{}$	$\boxed{}$	$\boxed{}$	$\boxed{}$	$\boxed{}$	$\boxed{}$

| 1 | 2 | 3 | 4 | 5 | 6 | 7 | 8 | 9 | 10 | 11 | 12 | 13 | 14 | 15 | 16 | 17 | 18 | 19 | 20 |

$$6 + 4 + 5 = \boxed{15}$$

3. $2 + 8 + 4 = \boxed{}$ $9 + 1 + 5 = \boxed{}$ $7 + 3 + 5 = \boxed{}$

$6 + 4 + 4 = \boxed{}$ $4 + 6 + 4 = \boxed{}$ $5 + 5 + 5 = \boxed{}$

$5 + 4 + 6 = \boxed{}$ $4 + 7 + 3 = \boxed{}$ $6 + 3 + 6 = \boxed{}$

$6 + 3 + 5 = \boxed{}$ $7 + 1 + 7 = \boxed{}$ $8 + 3 + 4 = \boxed{}$

Strand: Number
Curriculum Objectives:
Develop an understanding of addition by combining or partitioning sets, use concrete materials 0–20;
explore, develop and apply the commutative, associative and zero properties of addition;
develop and recall mental strategies for addition facts within 20;
construct number sentences and number stories;
solve problems involving addition within 20;
add numbers without renaming within 99.

Add

| 1 | 2 | 3 | 4 | 5 | 6 | 7 | 8 | 9 | 10 | 11 | 12 | 13 | 14 | 15 | 16 |

1. Circle the sums that equal the number under the apple.

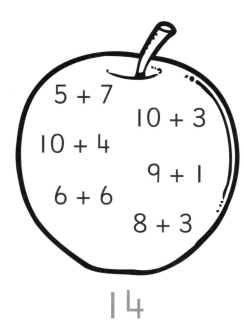

5 + 7
10 + 3
10 + 4
9 + 1
6 + 6
8 + 3

14

6 + 10
7 + 8
10 + 2
11 + 4
4 + 9
11 + 1

15

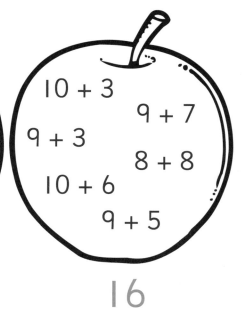

10 + 3
9 + 7
9 + 3
8 + 8
10 + 6
9 + 5

16

---

2. 9 + 7 = ☐   8 + 8 = ☐   11 + 4 = ☐   8 + 6 = ☐

   7 + 7 = ☐   9 + 6 = ☐   10 + 5 = ☐   2 + 13 = ☐

  12 + 4 = ☐   9 + 5 = ☐   10 + 6 = ☐   11 + 3 = ☐

3.
9	11	9	7	12	7	1	13	3
+5	+4	+6	+7	+2	+9	+13	+3	+12
☐	☐	☐	☐	☐	☐	☐	☐	☐

---

4. 10 + 4 + 1 = ☐   9 + 1 + 5 = ☐   8 + 4 + 2 = ☐

   9 + 4 + 1 = ☐   6 + 2 + 6 = ☐   7 + 4 + 4 = ☐

   5 + 5 + 5 = ☐   7 + 6 + 1 = ☐   6 + 4 + 4 = ☐

Seventeen

How many?
17
seventeen hurleys

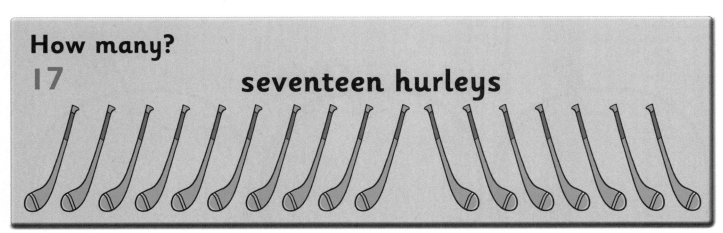

1. **Colour 1 square on the 10 block for every hurley.**

2. **Trace over the numeral 17.**

17 17 17 17 17 17 17 17 17

17 17 17 17 17 17 17 17 17

3. **Draw 17 socks**	4. **Draw 17 grapes**

5. seventeen   seventeen

28

Strand: Number
Curriculum Objectives:
count the number of objects in a set;

read, write and order numerals, 0–99;
estimate the number of objects in a set 0–20.

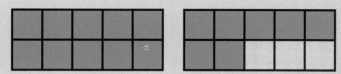

What makes 17?

seventeen

Here are 17 cubes and 2 plates.

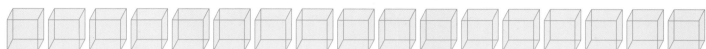

1. How many ways can you make 17?

☐ + ☐ = 17		☐ + ☐ = 17
☐ + ☐ = 17		☐ + ☐ = 17
☐ + ☐ = 17		☐ + ☐ = 17
☐ + ☐ = 17		☐ + ☐ = 17
☐ + ☐ = 17		☐ + ☐ = 17
☐ + ☐ = 17		☐ + ☐ = 17
☐ + ☐ = 17		☐ + ☐ = 17
☐ + ☐ = 17		☐ + ☐ = 17
☐ + ☐ = 17		☐ + ☐ = 17

Eighteen

How many?

18   **eighteen hedgehogs**

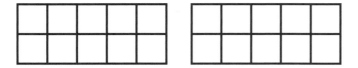

1. **Colour 1 square on the 10 frame for every hedgehog.**

2. **Trace over the numeral 18.**

3. **Draw 18 apples**	4. **Draw 18 kiwi fruit**

5. eighteen eighteen eighteen

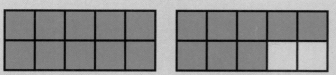
Here are 18 cubes and 2 plates.

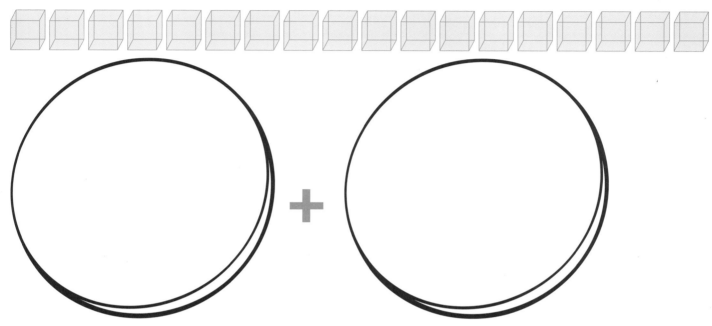

1. **How many ways can you make 18?**

☐ + ☐ = 18			☐ + ☐ = 18		
☐ + ☐ = 18			☐ + ☐ = 18		
☐ + ☐ = 18			☐ + ☐ = 18		
☐ + ☐ = 18			☐ + ☐ = 18		
☐ + ☐ = 18			☐ + ☐ = 18		
☐ + ☐ = 18			☐ + ☐ = 18		
☐ + ☐ = 18			☐ + ☐ = 18		
☐ + ☐ = 18			☐ + ☐ = 18		
☐ + ☐ = 18			☐ + ☐ = 18		
☐ + ☐ = 18					

Nineteen

How many?

19   **nineteen dogs**

1. **Colour 1 square on the 10 frame for every dog.**

2. **Trace over the numeral 19.**

3. Draw 19 bowls 	4. Draw 19 doors

5. nineteen nineteen nineteen

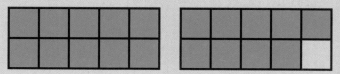

What makes 19?

nineteen

Here are 19 cubes and 2 plates.

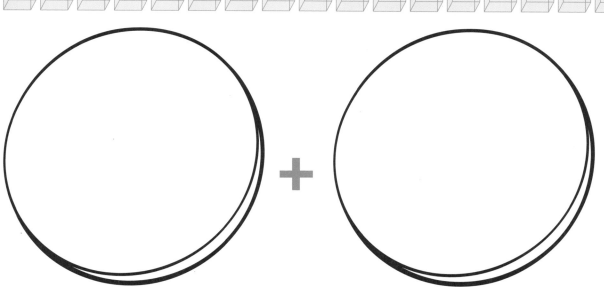

+

1. **How many ways can you make 19?**

☐ + ☐ = 19			☐ + ☐ = 19
☐ + ☐ = 19			☐ + ☐ = 19
☐ + ☐ = 19			☐ + ☐ = 19
☐ + ☐ = 19			☐ + ☐ = 19
☐ + ☐ = 19			☐ + ☐ = 19
☐ + ☐ = 19			☐ + ☐ = 19
☐ + ☐ = 19			☐ + ☐ = 19
☐ + ☐ = 19			☐ + ☐ = 19
☐ + ☐ = 19			☐ + ☐ = 19
☐ + ☐ = 19			☐ + ☐ = 19

Twenty

How many?
20   twenty rabbits

1. Colour 1 square on the 10 frame for every rabbit.

2. Trace over the numeral 20.

20 20 20 20 20 20 20

20 20 20 20 20 20 20

3. Draw 20 sweets 	4. Draw 20 bars

5. twenty   twenty   twenty

What makes 20?

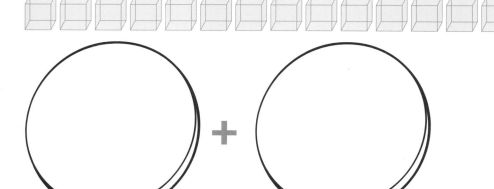

twenty

Here are 20 cubes and 2 plates.

1. **How many ways can you make 20?**

	+		= 20		+		= 20		+		= 20
	+		= 20		+		= 20		+		= 20
	+		= 20		+		= 20		+		= 20
	+		= 20		+		= 20		+		= 20
	+		= 20		+		= 20		+		= 20
	+		= 20		+		= 20		+		= 20
	+		= 20		+		= 20		+		= 20

Recap
- I can recognise, read and write numbers to 20.
- I can add numbers up to 20.
- I can work out the answers to story sums up to 20.

8. Addition 4

| 1 | 2 | 3 | 4 | 5 | 6 | 7 | 8 | 9 | 10 | 11 | 12 | 13 | 14 | 15 | 16 | 17 | 18 | 19 | 20 |

6 + 11 = 17

1. Count on, using the number strip.

14 + 4 = ☐ 9 + 8 = ☐ 15 + 3 = ☐ 10 + 7 = ☐

16 + 2 = ☐ 13 + 4 = ☐ 12 + 5 = ☐ 11 + 6 = ☐

8 + 10 = ☐ 12 + 6 = ☐ 13 + 4 = ☐ 9 + 9 = ☐

2.

8	15	7	16	12	9	15	13	10	11
+9	+ 3	+10	+ 2	+ 5	+ 9	+ 3	+ 4	+ 8	+ 7
☐	☐	☐	☐	☐	☐	☐	☐	☐	☐

| 1 | 2 | 3 | 4 | 5 | 6 | 7 | 8 | 9 | 10 | 11 | 12 | 13 | 14 | 15 | 16 | 17 | 18 | 19 | 20 |

3. 5 + 5 + 8 = ☐   9 + 1 + 7 = ☐   7 + 3 + 7 = ☐

    6 + 4 + 8 = ☐   4 + 6 + 8 = ☐   8 + 2 + 7 = ☐

    5 + 9 + 3 = ☐   4 + 10 + 7 = ☐   12 + 3 + 3 = ☐

    6 + 8 + 4 = ☐   7 + 8 + 3 = ☐   8 + 3 + 6 = ☐

Strand: Number
Curriculum Objectives:
Develop an understanding of addition by combining or partitioning sets, use concrete materials 0–20;
explore, develop and apply the commutative, associative and zero properties of addition;

develop and recall mental strategies for addition facts within 20;
construct number sentences and number stories;
solve problems involving addition within 20;
add numbers without and with renaming within 99;
explore and discuss repeated addition and group counting.

Add

| 1 | 2 | 3 | 4 | 5 | 6 | 7 | 8 | 9 | 10 | 11 | 12 | 13 | 14 | 15 | 16 | 17 | 18 | 19 | 20 |

1. Circle the sums that equal the numbers under the apple.

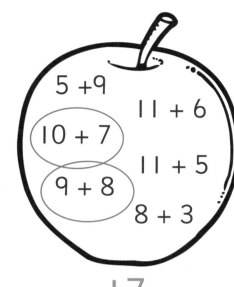

5 + 9
11 + 6
10 + 7
11 + 5
9 + 8
8 + 3

17

6 + 12
7 + 8
10 + 2
11 + 7
9 + 9
11 + 3

18

12 + 3
9 + 10
15 + 4
11 + 8
10 + 6
9 + 5

19

2.

$9 + 8 =$ ☐ $8 + 11 =$ ☐ $15 + 4 =$ ☐ $8 + 9 =$ ☐

$7 + 11 =$ ☐ $9 + 9 =$ ☐ $10 + 7 =$ ☐ $5 + 13 =$ ☐

$12 + 6 =$ ☐ $14 + 5 =$ ☐ $10 + 9 =$ ☐ $11 + 6 =$ ☐

$12 + 5 =$ ☐ $6 + 13 =$ ☐ $2 + 16 =$ ☐ $14 + 3 =$ ☐

3.

9	11	12	9	11	12	8	7	1
+ 8	+ 7	+ 6	+ 9	+ 6	+ 5	+10	+12	+16
☐	☐	☐	☐	☐	☐	☐	☐	☐

4. Find the total.

$10 + 4 + 3 =$ ☐ $9 + 1 + 7 =$ ☐ $8 + 8 + 2 =$ ☐

$9 + 4 + 4 =$ ☐ $6 + 6 + 6 =$ ☐ $7 + 7 + 5 =$ ☐

$5 + 5 + 8 =$ ☐ $7 + 6 + 6 =$ ☐ $6 + 7 + 4 =$ ☐

Addition to 20

1	2	3	4	5	6	7	8	9	10	11	12	13	14	15	16	17	18	19	20

1. **Count on, using the number strip.**

7 + 4 = ☐   16 + 4 = ☐   5 + 8 = ☐   10 + 7 = ☐

6 + 9 = ☐   13 + 7 = ☐   12 + 8 = ☐   11 + 9 = ☐

8 + 8 = ☐   15 + 5 = ☐   17 + 3 = ☐   7 + 9 = ☐

2.
10	8	11	15	9	18	19	10	14	13
+10	+ 9	+ 9	+ 6	+10	+ 2	+ 1	+ 9	+ 6	+ 6
☐	☐	☐	☐	☐	☐	☐	☐	☐	☐

3. **Use the number strip to do these.**

5 + 5 + 9 = ☐   9 + 1 + 10 = ☐   7 + 3 + 8 = ☐

6 + 4 + 8 = ☐   4 + 6 + 10 = ☐   8 + 2 + 9 = ☐

5 + 4 + 9 = ☐   4 + 8 + 8 = ☐   12 + 3 + 4 = ☐

13 + 3 + 2 = ☐   7 + 7 + 6 = ☐   8 + 3 + 8 = ☐

7 + 9 + 4 = ☐   9 + 1 + 9 = ☐   10 + 0 + 10 = ☐

7 + 8 + 5 = ☐   9 + 1 + 10 = ☐   10 + 1 + 8 = ☐

4. **Ross has 6 crayons, Ben has 7 crayons and Dan has 5 crayons. What is the total number of crayons? ☐
Draw the crayons.**

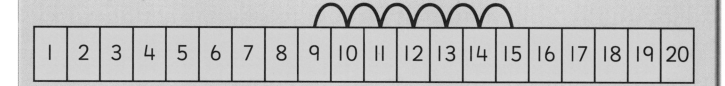

9 + [?] = 15   Start at 9 and count the steps to get to 15.

It takes 6 steps, so 9 + 6 = 15

| 1 | 2 | 3 | 4 | 5 | 6 | 7 | 8 | 9 | 10 | 11 | 12 | 13 | 14 | 15 | 16 | 17 | 18 | 19 | 20 |

1. **Find the total.**

7 + [ ] = 14   6 + [ ] = 13   11 + [ ] = 16   9 + [ ] = 13

15 + [ ] = 19   18 + [ ] = 20   8 + [ ] = 16   13 + [ ] = 18

14 + [ ] = 16   10 + [ ] = 19   10 + [ ] = 17   9 + [ ] = 19

2. **Circle the sums that equal 20.**

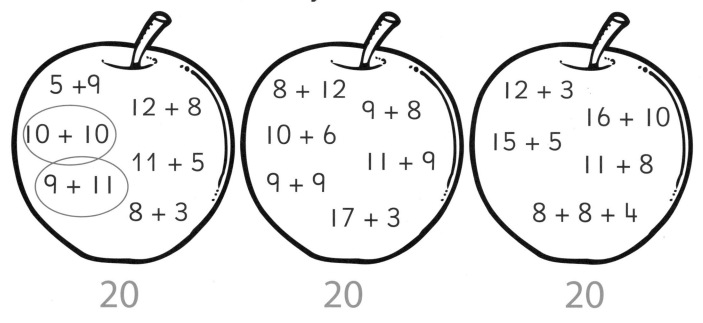

5 + 9
12 + 8
(10 + 10)
11 + 5
(9 + 11)
8 + 3

20

8 + 12
9 + 8
10 + 6
11 + 9
9 + 9
17 + 3

20

12 + 3
16 + 10
15 + 5
11 + 8
8 + 8 + 4

20

3. **The farmer put 12 cows in the field in the morning. She put 8 more in the field in the afternoon.**

   How many cows are in the field now? [ ]

4. **There are 9 goats under the tree, 6 goats near the river and 5 goats in the barn.**

   How many goats does the farmer have? [ ]

Double Up to 10

1. Match to the correct balloon.

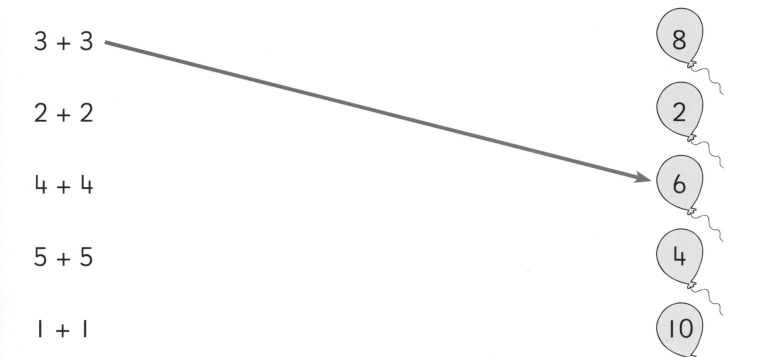

3 + 3

2 + 2

4 + 4

5 + 5

1 + 1

8

2

6

4

10

2. Add the numbers in the balloons.

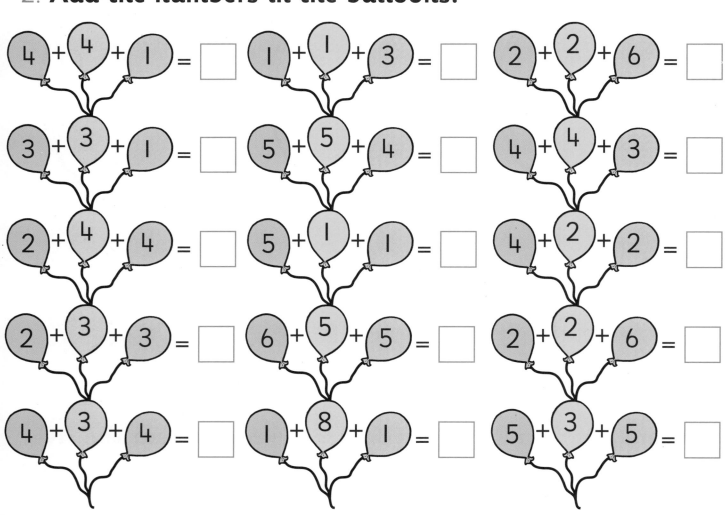

4 + 4 + 1 = ☐

1 + 1 + 3 = ☐

2 + 2 + 6 = ☐

3 + 3 + 1 = ☐

5 + 5 + 4 = ☐

4 + 4 + 3 = ☐

2 + 4 + 4 = ☐

5 + 1 + 1 = ☐

4 + 2 + 2 = ☐

2 + 3 + 3 = ☐

6 + 5 + 5 = ☐

2 + 2 + 6 = ☐

4 + 3 + 4 = ☐

1 + 8 + 1 = ☐

5 + 3 + 5 = ☐

Double Up to 20

1. Match to the correct balloon.

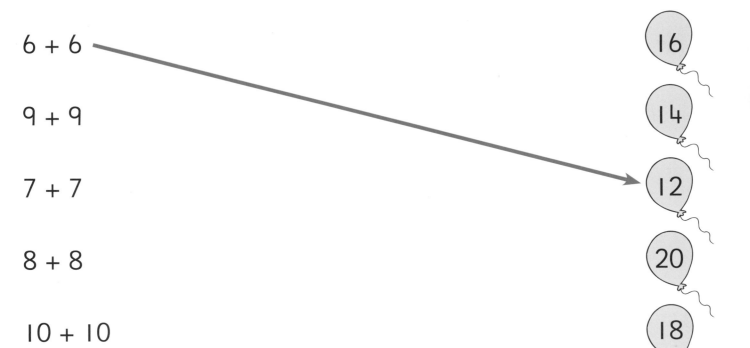

6 + 6

9 + 9

7 + 7

8 + 8

10 + 10

16

14

12

20

18

2. Add the numbers in the balloons.

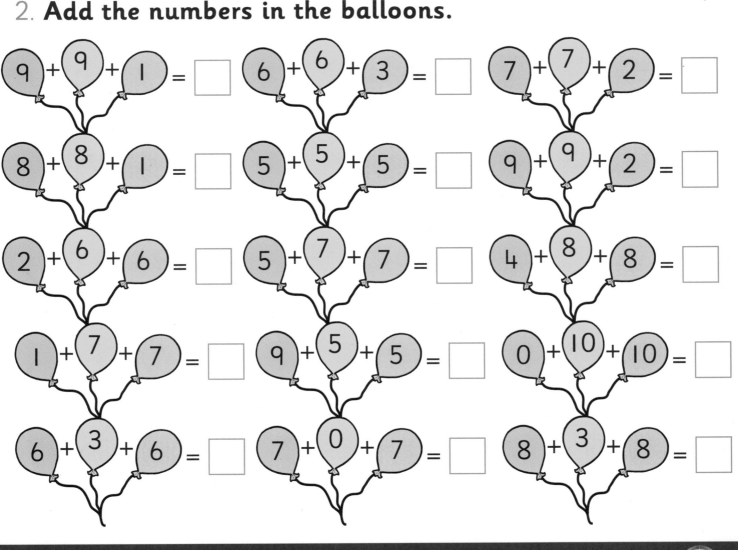

9 + 9 + 1 = ☐   6 + 6 + 3 = ☐   7 + 7 + 2 = ☐

8 + 8 + 1 = ☐   5 + 5 + 5 = ☐   9 + 9 + 2 = ☐

2 + 6 + 6 = ☐   5 + 7 + 7 = ☐   4 + 8 + 8 = ☐

1 + 7 + 7 = ☐   9 + 5 + 5 = ☐   0 + 10 + 10 = ☐

6 + 3 + 6 = ☐   7 + 0 + 7 = ☐   8 + 3 + 8 = ☐

Double Up

1. Write the missing number.

$$
\begin{array}{r} 3 \\ + \boxed{} \\ \hline 6 \end{array}
\qquad
\begin{array}{r} 2 \\ + 2 \\ \hline \boxed{} \end{array}
\qquad
\begin{array}{r} 4 \\ + \boxed{} \\ \hline 8 \end{array}
\qquad
\begin{array}{r} 5 \\ + 5 \\ \hline \boxed{} \end{array}
\qquad
\begin{array}{r} 4 \\ + 4 \\ \hline \boxed{} \end{array}
$$

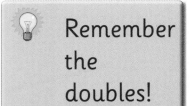
Remember the doubles!

$$
\begin{array}{r} 6 \\ + \boxed{} \\ \hline 12 \end{array}
\qquad
\begin{array}{r} 7 \\ + 7 \\ \hline \boxed{} \end{array}
\qquad
\begin{array}{r} 8 \\ + \boxed{} \\ \hline 16 \end{array}
\qquad
\begin{array}{r} 9 \\ + 9 \\ \hline \boxed{} \end{array}
\qquad
\begin{array}{r} 10 \\ + \boxed{} \\ \hline 20 \end{array}
$$

2. Write the missing number.

$4 + \boxed{} = 8$ $5 + \boxed{} = 10$ $7 + \boxed{} = 14$

$3 + \boxed{} = 6$ $6 + \boxed{} = 12$ $8 + \boxed{} = 16$

$9 + \boxed{} = 18$ $10 + \boxed{} = 20$ $2 + \boxed{} = 4$

3. Add the numbers in the balloons.

 $4 + 4 + 5 = \boxed{}$

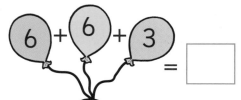 $6 + 6 + 3 = \boxed{}$

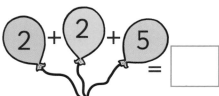 $2 + 2 + 5 = \boxed{}$

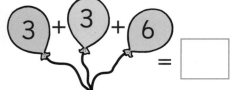 $3 + 3 + 6 = \boxed{}$

 $5 + 5 + 9 = \boxed{}$

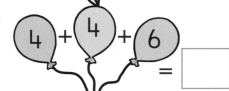 $4 + 4 + 6 = \boxed{}$

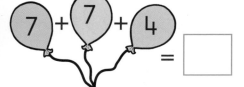 $7 + 7 + 4 = \boxed{}$

 $8 + 8 + 1 = \boxed{}$

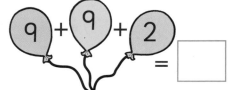 $9 + 9 + 2 = \boxed{}$

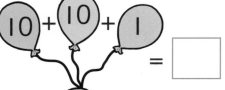 $10 + 10 + 1 = \boxed{}$

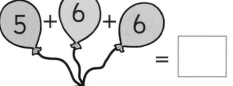 $5 + 6 + 6 = \boxed{}$

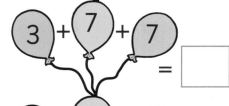 $3 + 7 + 7 = \boxed{}$

$8 + 3 + 8 = \boxed{}$

$9 + 1 + 9 = \boxed{}$

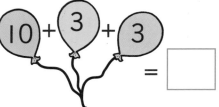 $10 + 3 + 3 = \boxed{}$

Double Up

When you know your doubles, other sums are easier to do.

doubles

1. $2 + 2 = \boxed{}$

2. $3 + 3 = \boxed{}$

3. $4 + 4 = \boxed{}$

4. $5 + 5 = \boxed{}$

5. $6 + 6 = \boxed{}$

6. $7 + 7 = \boxed{}$

7. $8 + 8 = \boxed{}$

8. $9 + 9 = \boxed{}$

near doubles

$2 + 3 = \boxed{}$
$2 + 2 + 1 = \boxed{}$

$3 + 4 = \boxed{}$
$3 + 3 + 1 = \boxed{}$

$4 + 5 = \boxed{}$
$4 + 4 + 1 = \boxed{}$

$5 + 6 = \boxed{}$
$5 + 5 + 1 = \boxed{}$

$6 + 7 = \boxed{}$
$6 + 6 + 1 = \boxed{}$

$7 + 8 = \boxed{}$
$7 + 7 + 1 = \boxed{}$

$8 + 9 = \boxed{}$
$8 + 8 + 1 = \boxed{}$

$9 + 10 = \boxed{}$
$9 + 9 + 1 = \boxed{}$

Add the numbers in the flags.

Look for the numbers that make 10 to make it easy.

7 + 3 = 10 so 7 + 3 + 2 = 12

1. **Try these. Remember to find 10 first.**

 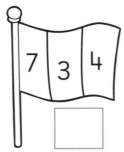 

 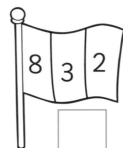  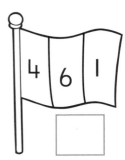

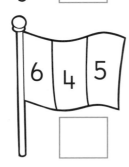   

2. 2 + 2 + 8 = ☐   4 + 6 + 4 = ☐   5 + 8 + 5 = ☐

    3 + 7 + 5 = ☐   1 + 7 + 9 = ☐   10 + 9 + 0 = ☐

    3 + 9 + 7 = ☐   9 + 1 + 8 = ☐   6 + 4 + 7 = ☐

    5 + 5 + 1 = ☐   8 + 2 + 3 = ☐   7 + 3 + 5 = ☐

    9 + 8 + 2 = ☐   7 + 9 + 1 = ☐   8 + 4 + 6 = ☐

Now we know that
5 + 4 = 4 + 5   or   2 + 9 = 9 + 2.
We can use this to make us quicker at our addition.
It is easier to start with the bigger number.
11 + 3 is easier than 3 + 11 as we only have to count on 3.

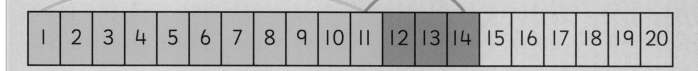

| 1 | 2 | 3 | 4 | 5 | 6 | 7 | 8 | 9 | 10 | 11 | 12 | 13 | 14 | 15 | 16 | 17 | 18 | 19 | 20 |

Now try these. Start with the bigger number.

1.   2 + 7 = ☐   11 + 4 = ☐   15 + 5 = ☐

   6 + 12 = ☐   12 + 4 = ☐   3 + 17 = ☐

   4 + 10 = ☐   14 + 2 = ☐   3 + 16 = ☐

2.   9 + 8 = ☐   8 + 11 = ☐   15 + 5 = ☐

   8 + 9 = ☐   9 + 11 = ☐   9 + 10 = ☐

   10 + 7 = ☐   13 + 7 = ☐   12 + 7 = ☐

3.
9	11	12	7	11	7	12	7	8	7	1	14
+9	+9	+8	+9	+6	+12	+5	+12	+10	+12	+19	+3
☐	☐	☐	☐	☐	☐	☐	☐	☐	☐	☐	☐

 Look out for:
   • the numbers that make 10.
   • the doubles and near doubles.

4.   10 + 7 + 3 = ☐   9 + 1 + 8 = ☐

   9 + 4 + 4 = ☐   6 + 6 + 8 = ☐

   5 + 5 + 8 = ☐   7 + 6 + 6 = ☐

Problem Solving

Write an addition sentence.

💡 Use your cubes, beads or counters to help you do these sums.

1.

There are 9 party bags on the table. Mammy is filling 9 more party bags. How many party bags are there in total?

| 9 | + | 9 | = | |

2.

There are 12 buns in the box. There are 5 buns on the plate. How many buns are there altogether?

| | + | | = | |

3.

Mammy has 7 red party plates. Daddy has 13 blue party plates. How many plates have they in total?

| | + | | = | |

4.

6 boys are playing football. 8 are on the bouncy castle. 3 are eating cake. How many boys are at the party?

| | + | | + | | = | |

Recap
- I can add numbers to 20.
- I can 'count on' using number strips.
- I know my doubles and near doubles to 20.
- I can use lots of ways to solve addition problems to 20.

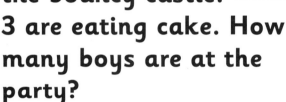

9. 2-D Shapes

1. **Colour the triangle.**

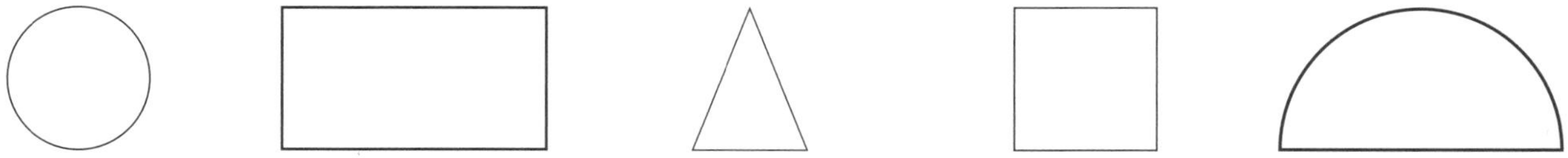

2. **Colour the square.**

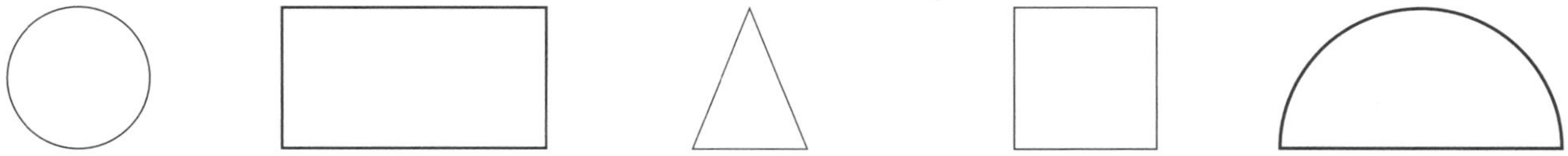

3. **Colour the rectangle.**

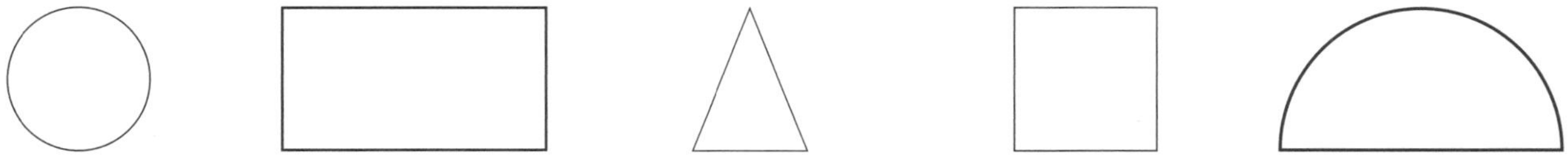

4. **Write the missing word.**

| square | circle | triangle | rectangle | semi-circle |

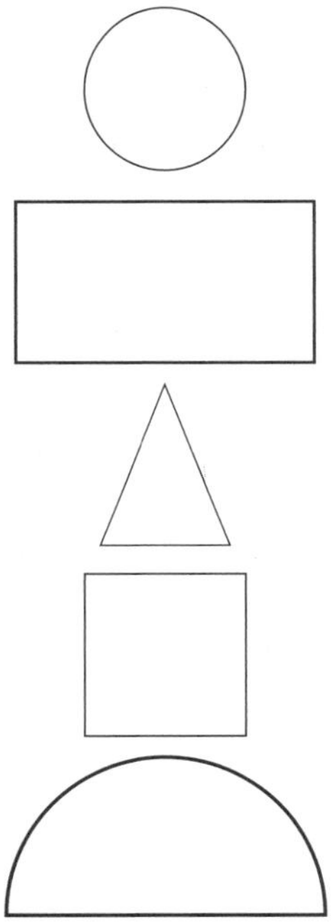

This shape is a [____]

This shape is a [____]

This shape is a [____]

This shape is a [____]

This shape is a [____]

Art Time –
Semi-circle-
osaurus!

Cut out lots of
semi-circles of
different sizes.
You can stick the
semi-circles together
to form a dinosaur.

Strand: Shape and Space
Curriculum Objectives:
Name and describe 2-D shapes;
draw 2-D shapes and identify them from their properties;
identify 2-D shapes in the environment.

47

1. Draw the shapes.

square

circle

triangle

rectangle

semi-circle

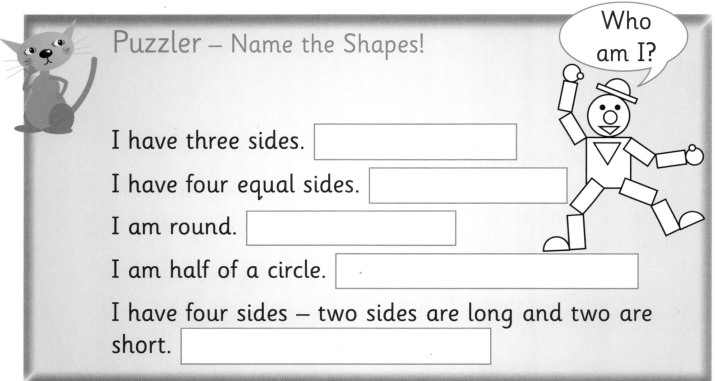

Puzzler – Name the Shapes!

Who am I?

I have three sides. _____

I have four equal sides. _____

I am round. _____

I am half of a circle. _____

I have four sides – two sides are long and two are short. _____

Recap

- I know about circles, semi-circles, triangles, squares and rectangles.
- I know how many sides each shape has.

○ ○ ○
○ ○ ○

10. Place Value 1

1.

Count the lollipops ☐
Colour 10
12 = 10 + 2

2.

Count the sunflowers ☐
Colour 10
14 = 10 + ☐

3.

Count the puppies ☐
Colour 10
15 = 10 + ☐

4.

Count the cars ☐
Colour 10
17 = 10 + ☐

5.

Count the pencils ☐
Colour 10
11 = 10 + ☐

6.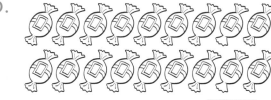

Count the sweets ☐
Colour 10
18 = 10 + ☐

7.

Count the ice lollies ☐
Colour 10
13 = 10 + ☐

8.

Count the schoolbags ☐
Colour 10
☐ = 10 + ☐

Strand: Number

Curriculum Objective:
Explore, identify and record place value 0–99.

49

Tens and Units

1.

Count the footballs ☐

Circle 10 footballs

14 = 10 + 4

14 = 1 ten and 4 units

2.

Count the hats ☐

Circle 10 hats

16 = 10 + ☐

16 = ☐ ten and ☐ units

3.

Count the trucks ☐

Circle 10 trucks

11 = 10 + ☐

11 = ☐ ten and ☐ unit

4.

Count the trees ☐

Circle 10 trees

17 = 10 + ☐

17 = ☐ ten and ☐ units

5.

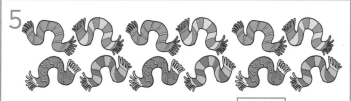

Count the scarves ☐

Circle 10 scarves

12 = 10 + ☐

12 = ☐ ten and ☐ units

6.

Count the bikes ☐

Circle 10 bikes

15 = 10 + ☐

15 = ☐ ten and ☐ units

7. Now try these:

a) 11 = ☐ ten and ☐ units   b) 19 = ☐ ten and ☐ units

c) 15 = ☐ ten and ☐ units   d) 14 = ☐ ten and ☐ units

e) 17 = ☐ ten and ☐ units   f) 16 = ☐ ten and ☐ units

g) 12 = ☐ ten and ☐ units   h) 1 = ☐ ten and ☐ units

Tens and Units

1.

How many apples altogether?

10 + 3 = 13

1 ten + 3 units = 13

2.

How many marbles altogether?

10 + ☐ = ☐

1 ten + ☐ units = ☐

3.

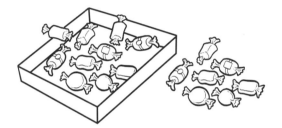

How many sweets altogether?

☐ + ☐ = ☐

☐ ten + ☐ units = ☐

4.

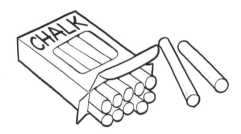

How many chalks altogether?

☐ + ☐ = ☐

☐ ten + ☐ units = ☐

5.

How many socks altogether?

☐ + ☐ = ☐

☐ ten + ☐ units = ☐

6.

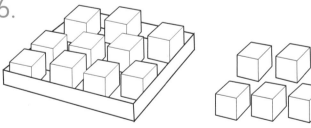

How many blocks altogether?

☐ + ☐ = ☐

☐ ten + ☐ units = ☐

Use cubes to help you answer these questions.

1.

There are 12 cubes.

Stack 10 cubes together.
How many cubes are left?

1 ten + 2 units = 12

2.

There are 15 cubes.

Stack 10 cubes together.
How many cubes are left?

1 ten + ☐ units = ☐

3.

There are 11 cubes.

Stack 10 cubes together.
How many cubes are left?

1 ten + ☐ units = ☐

4.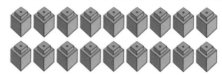

There are 18 cubes.

Stack 10 cubes together.
How many cubes are left?

1 ten + ☐ units = ☐

5.

There are 19 cubes.

Stack 10 cubes together.
How many cubes are left?

1 ten + ☐ units = ☐

6.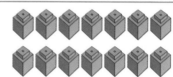

There are 14 cubes.

Stack 10 cubes together.
How many cubes are left?

1 ten + ☐ units = ☐

7.

There are 13 cubes.

Stack 10 cubes together.
How many cubes are left?

1 ten + ☐ units = ☐

8.

There are 17 cubes.

Stack 10 cubes together.
How many cubes are left?

1 ten + ☐ units = ☐

30 thirty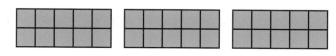

1. Write the number and the word.

30 30 30 30 thirty thirty

2. Fill in the missing numbers on the stepping stones.

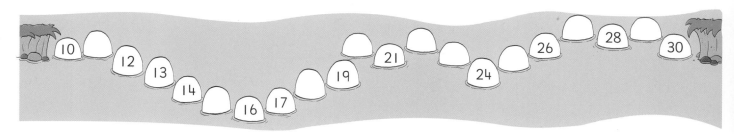

3. What comes before and after these numbers?

	22			25			27	
	29			21			26	

4. What number is on my t-shirt?

Look at the clues and cross out the numbers that are not on my t-shirt.

16   25   29   22   24   28   27

- It is more than 20.
- It is less than 25.
- It is not 20 + 4.
- It is an even number.

Now write the number on my t-shirt.

40 forty

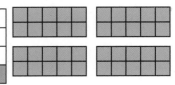

1. Write the number and the word.

40   40   40   40   forty   forty

2. Write the numbers that come before and after these numbers.

	20				28					40		20		
37					36					39		38		

3. Fill in the missing numbers.

1	2	3	4		6	7		9	10
11		13		15	16		18	19	
21	22		24	25		27	28		30
	32	33		35	36		38		

4. Cross out the numbers that are not on my t-shirt.

19   34   25   36   29   38   22   31   27   33

- It is more than 20.
- It is less than 35.
- It has more than two tens.
- It is not an odd number.

Now write the number on my t-shirt.

50 fifty

1	2	3	4	5	6	7	8	9	10
11	12	13	14	15	16	17	18	19	20
21	22	23	24	25	26	27	28	29	30
31	32	33	34	35	36	37	38	39	40
41	42	43	44	45	46	47	48	49	50

ten
twenty
thirty
forty
fifty

1. **Fill in the missing numbers.**

Count forward ➡ one step each time.

4	5	6	7		

12	13	14	15		

15	16	17			

28	29	30			

24	25	26			

27	28	29			

31		33		35	

43		45		47	

2. **What comes after...?**

4

49

15

21

33

46

1. **Match each of these numerals to the correct word.**

37 ————————————————————————→ twenty-five

26   forty-seven

15   thirty-seven

25   thirty

40   twenty-six

38   fifty

30   thirty-eight

29   fifteen

50   twenty-nine

47   forty

2. **Write the words.**

10 = _____   20 = _____

30 = _____   40 = _____

50 = _____   17 = _____

23 = _____   35 = _____

48 = _____   59 = _____

12. Algebra – Extending and Using Patterns

 Can you remember how to make a pattern?

1. Complete the pattern below.

2. Finish this pattern.

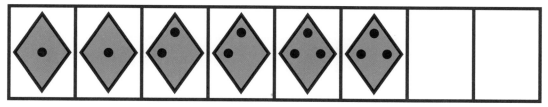

3. Now make your own pattern.

Number Patterns – Odd and Even

The numbers in red are **even**, the numbers in blue are **odd**.

1	2	3	4	5	6	7	8	9	10

4. The odd numbers are ☐ , ☐ , ☐ , ☐ , ☐ .

The even numbers are ☐ , ☐ , ☐ , ☐ , ☐ .

Poem Time
Zero, two, four, six, eight – being **even** is just great.
One, three, five, seven, nine – being **odd** is just fine.

Strand: Algebra

Curriculum Objectives:
Explore and use patterns in addition facts;
recognise pattern, including odd and even numbers.

Sock Solver!

Mammy is not happy. Some socks are missing from the washing machine.

1. **Colour the socks to make pairs. ✓ the correct box. See if there are any left over.**

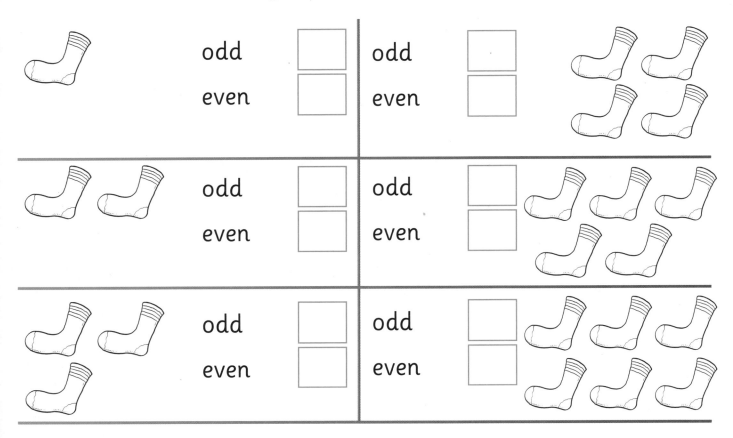

	odd ☐	odd ☐	
	even	even	
	odd ☐	odd ☐	
	even	even	
	odd ☐	odd ☐	
	even	even	

2. **Colour the odd numbers red. Colour the even numbers green.**

2	1	3	8
5	4	10	7
9	12	6	11

Recap
- I can recognise and complete a pattern.
- I know odd and even numbers.

13. Data

Sort

1. **Count the toys, containers and clothes.**
Colour and match.

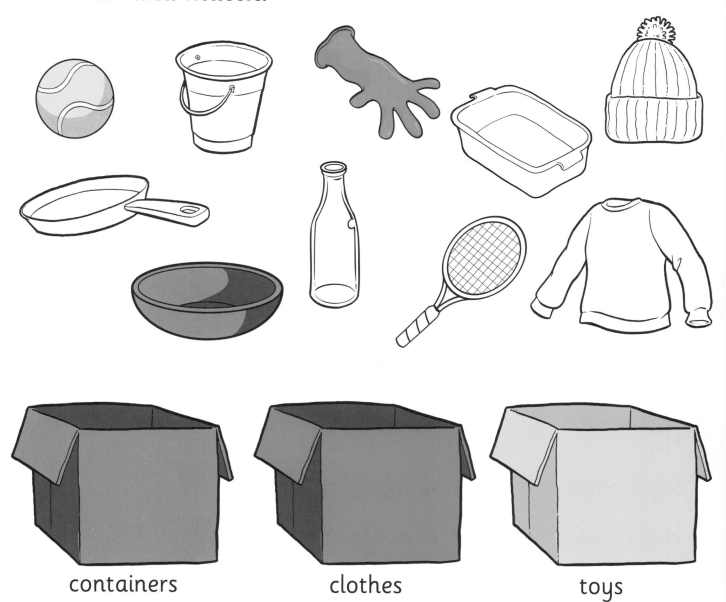

containers   clothes   toys

2. **Now answer these questions:**

a) How many toys? ☐

b) How many containers? ☐

c) How many items of clothing? ☐

Strand: Data
Curriculum Objectives:
Sort and classify objects by two and three criteria;

represent and interpret data in two, three or four rows or
columns using real objects, models and pictures.

Treat Day!

Here are the treats the children at Aoife's party chose.

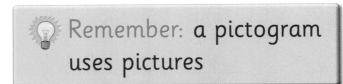

Remember: a pictogram uses pictures

crisps	sweets	chocolate bar

1. **How many chose crisps** ? ☐

2. **How many chose sweets** ? ☐

3. **How many chose a chocolate bar** ? ☐

4. **True or false?**

   a) Chocolate was the least popular treat _____

   b) Crisps were the most popular treat _____

   c) The same number of children like sweets as like crisps _____

   d) 7 children altogether like chocolate_____

   e) More children like crisps than like sweets _____

   f) 3 more children like chocolate than like sweets _____

Tidy Your Room!

1. **Count and colour the correct number of blocks. How many?**

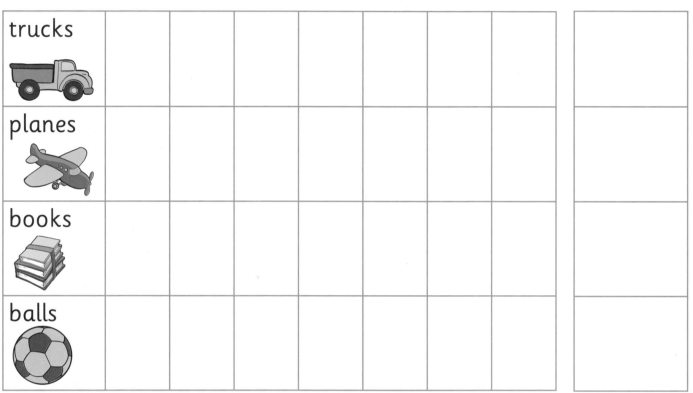

trucks								
planes								
books								
balls								

2. a) How many objects are there altogether? ☐

   b) How many trucks and planes are there altogether? ☐

   c) How many more balls than planes? ☐

   d) How many fewer trucks than balls? ☐

Recap
• I know what a pictogram is and I can use
  pictograms to organise and record data. ○ ○ ○

1. **Can you perform these tasks before the sand runs through a one-minute timer? Colour the correct box.**

   a) Your class can sing a song   Yes   or   No

   b) You can stack 20 cubes   Yes   or   No

   c) You can do 30 star jumps   Yes   or   No

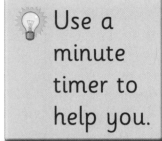

💡 Use a minute timer to help you.

2. **What can you do in one minute?**

How far can you count? ☐	How many pages in your English book can you read? ☐	How many animals can you name? (Cat, dog, tiger...) ☐
Can you say the alphabet? ☐	How many times can you write your name in your copy? ☐	How many times can you hop on one foot? ☐

Challenge

How many days in 2 weeks?   ☐ + ☐ = ☐

How many days in 3 weeks?   ☐ + ☐ + ☐ = ☐

Strand: Measures
Curriculum Objectives:
Use the vocabulary of time to sequence events;
read and record time using simple devices;
read day, date and month using calendar.

Days of the Week

1 Sunday	2 Monday	3 Tuesday	4 Wednesday	5 Thursday	6 Friday	7 Saturday

1. **There are** ☐ **days in a week.**

2. **The first day is** ☐.

3. **The sixth day is** ☐.

4. **The last day is** ☐.

5. **Today is** ☐.

6. **Yesterday was** ☐.

7. **Tomorrow will be** ☐.

8. **The day after Tuesday is** ☐.

Sunday Monday Tuesday Wednesday Thursday Friday Saturday

9. **Chewie the dog had a bath on** ☐.

10. **He dug a hole on** ☐.

11. **He played ball on** ☐.

12. **He went for a walk on** ☐.

13. **He chewed a bone on** ☐.

14. **On** ☐ **he chased a cat.**

15. **On** ☐ **he got a stick.**

Months

1. January
2. February
3. March
4. April
5. May
6. June
7. July
8. August
9. September
10. October
11. November
12. December

1. **How many months in a year?** ☐

2. **Now it is the month of** ☐.

3. **Last month was** ☐.

4. **Next month will be** ☐.

5. **The second month is** ☐.

6. **The tenth month is** ☐.

7. **February comes after** ☐.

8. **October comes before** ☐.

9. **My birthday is in the month of** ☐.

10. **In which month would you see:**

☐

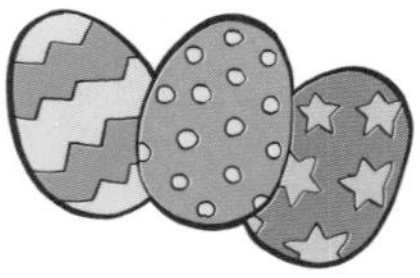

☐

☐

☐

Seasons

There are four seasons. Each season has three months.

Spring	**Summer**	**Autumn**	**Winter**

Spring		**Summer**	
• February • March • April		• May • June • July	
Autumn		**Winter**	
• August • September • October		• November • December • January	

1. There are ☐ seasons in a year.

2. Name the seasons:

3. There are ☐ months in each season.

4. March and April are in the season of _____.

5. Leaves fall from the trees in _____.

6. December is in the season of _____.

7. It is cold in the season of _____.

8. _____ is the hottest season.

9. Now it is the season of _____.

10. My favourite season is _____.

March						
Sunday	Monday	Tuesday	Wednesday	Thursday	Friday	Saturday
	1	2	3 ⚽	4	5	6
7	8	9	10	11	12	13
14	15	16	17	18	19	20
21	22	23	24	25	26	27
28	29	30	31			

1. **What day is the 1st of March?** _____

2. **What day is the last day of March?** _____

3. **How many Tuesdays in March?** ☐

4. **How many Fridays in March?** ☐

5. **What day does Megan play football?** _____

6. **Megan plays football on the** ☐ **rd of** _____

7. **What day is the 18th of March?** _____

8. **What date is the third Monday? It is the** ☐ **th of** ____

9. **Megan went to the library on the 29th of March. Tick ✓ this date.**

10. **Granny came to visit on the 24th of March. Tick ✓ this date.**

11. **Draw a shamrock 🍀 on the 17th of March.**

12. **Tick ✓ the weekends – Saturday and Sunday.**

13. **Monday 22nd of March was sunny. Draw a**

14. **Wednesday 10th of March was wet. Draw some**

Finished Early?

- Look up your birthday on a calendar.
- What **day** is your birthday this year? _____

15. Check-up 1

1	2	3	4	5	6	7	8	9	10	11	12	13	14	15	16	17	18	19	20

Try these:

1. $3 + 0 =$ ☐ $0 + 6 =$ ☐ $5 + 3 =$ ☐ $3 + 9 =$ ☐

2. $2 + 6 + 1 =$ ☐ $3 + 4 + 2 =$ ☐ $8 =$ ☐ $+$ ☐

3. **What numbers come next?**

15	16	17			

30	31	32			

4. **What shape am I?**

   I have 3 straight sides. I am a [   ].

   I am half a circle. I am a [   ].

5. $6 +$ ☐ $+ 2 = 10$ $4 + 3 +$ ☐ $= 12$ $2 + 7 +$ ☐ $= 11$

6.

1	2	3	4	5	6	7	8	9	10

   Colour odd numbers purple, even orange.

7. **What is the first day of the week?** [   ]

8. **What day comes before Friday?** [   ]

9. **It is the season of** [   ].

Curriculum Objective:
To revise concepts that were explored in units 2–14.

67

16. Subtraction 1

How Many Are Left?

10 crayons. Take away 3. How many are left?

$10 - 3 = \boxed{7}$

1. **8 sets of books. Take away 2. How many bundles are left?**

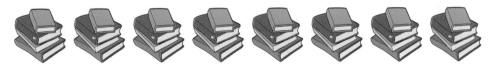

$8 - 2 = \boxed{}$

2. $5 - 1 = \boxed{}$

3. $7 - 4 = \boxed{}$

4. $9 - 5 = \boxed{}$

5. $8 - 4 = \boxed{}$

6. $\boxed{} - \boxed{} = \boxed{}$

7. $\boxed{} - \boxed{} = \boxed{}$

Strand: Number
Curriculum Objectives:
Develop an understanding of subtraction as deducting, as complementing and as difference 0–20;
develop and/or recall mental strategies for subtraction 0–20;
construct number sentences and number stories;
solve problems involving subtraction 0–20;
estimate differences within 99;
subtract numbers without renaming within 99;
use the symbols +, –, =;
solve one-step problems involving addition or subtraction.

Subtraction

6 pineapples. Take away 2. How many are left?

6 − 2 = 4

1.  8 − 3 = ☐

2. 7 − 4 = ☐

3. 4 − 2 = ☐

4. 9 − 6 = ☐

5. 8 − 5 = ☐

6. 9 − 5 = ☐

7.

10 − 7 = ☐

8. 7 − 4 = ☐

9. 6 − 5 = ☐

Counters

Try these. Use your counters to work out the answers.

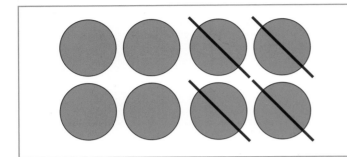

$$8 - 4 = \boxed{}$$

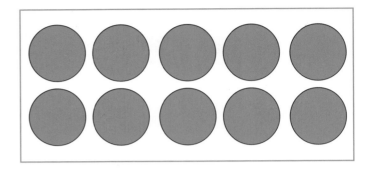

$$10 - 2 = \boxed{}$$

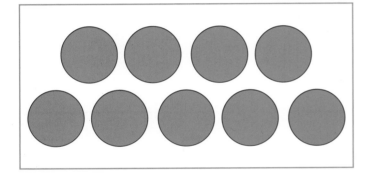

$$9 - 5 = \boxed{}$$

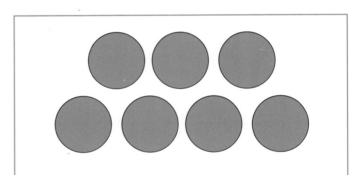

$$7 - 4 = \boxed{}$$

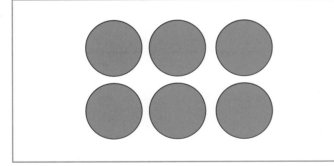

$$6 - 5 = \boxed{}$$

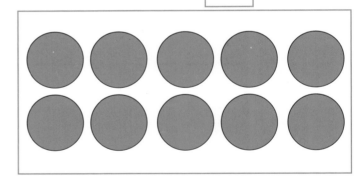

$$10 - 5 = \boxed{}$$

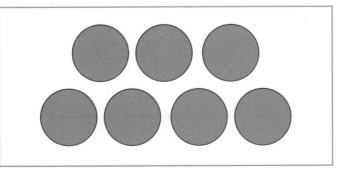

$$7 - 2 = \boxed{}$$

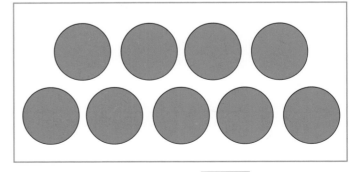

$$9 - 3 = \boxed{}$$

Subtraction

1. $9 - 8 = \boxed{}$

2. $8 - 6 = \boxed{}$

3. $6 - 2 = \boxed{}$

4. $6 - 3 = \boxed{}$

5. $9 - 5 = \boxed{}$

6. $7 - 5 = \boxed{}$

7. $5 - 1 = \boxed{}$

8. $10 - 3 = \boxed{}$

9. $7 - 4 = \boxed{}$

10. $9 - 6 = \boxed{}$

11. $10 - 8 = \boxed{}$

12. $4 - 3 = \boxed{}$

13. $8 - 5 = \boxed{}$

14. $3 - 2 = \boxed{}$

Subtraction

1. $10 - 5 =$ ☐

2. $7 - 6 =$ ☐

3. $9 - 4 =$ ☐

4. $4 - 2 =$ ☐

5. $10 - 2 =$ ☐

6. $8 - 8 =$ ☐

7. $5 - 4 =$ ☐

8. $4 - 1 =$ ☐

9. $7 - 1 =$ ☐

10. $9 - 9 =$ ☐

11. $10 - 7 =$ ☐

12. $10 - 1 =$ ☐

13. $2 - 1 =$ ☐

14. $8 - 4 =$ ☐

Subtraction

Joey starts on 8. He jumps back 3 spaces and lands on 5.
8 – 3 = 5

1	2	3	4	5	6	7	8	9	10	11	12	13	14	15	16	17	18	19	20

Use the number line to help you answer these sums.

1. 4 – 3 = ☐   9 – 9 = ☐   10 – 7 = ☐

2. 6 – 3 = ☐   10 – 8 = ☐   8 – 6 = ☐

3. 9 – 3 = ☐   4 – 2 = ☐   7 – 5 = ☐

4. 6 – 6 = ☐   5 – 1 = ☐   8 – 4 = ☐

5. 7 – 7 = ☐   4 – 1 = ☐   6 – 2 = ☐

6.
```
   7      5      8     10     9      8
 – 6    – 2    – 1    – 3   – 5    – 4
 ___    ___    ___    ___   ___    ___
```

7.
```
  10      9      8      5      8     10
 – 9    – 7    – 0    – 5    – 6    – 5
 ___    ___    ___    ___    ___    ___
```

Recap
- I know how to subtract numbers up to 10. ○ ○ ○
- I can use a number line to help subtract numbers. ○ ○ ○

17. Comparing and Ordering

More Than

1.  Jack

    Carol

   Carol has 2 **more basketballs than Jack.**

2. Tom

    Paul

   Tom has ☐ **more goldfish than Paul.**

3. Jane

    Sasha

   _____ **has** ☐ **more pencils than** _____.

4. Finbarr

    Bobby

   _____ **has** ☐ **more t-shirts than** _____.

Strand: Number
Curriculum Objectives:
Compare equivalent and non-equivalent sets 0–20;
order sets of objects by number;
use the language of ordinal number, first to tenth.

Less Than

1.

There are ☐ less elephants than giraffes.

2.

There are ☐ less kittens than monkeys.

3.

There are ☐ less pizzas than birthday cakes.

4.

There are ☐ less dragons than robots.

5.

There are ☐ less guinea pigs than tigers.

More Than – Less Than – Same Amount

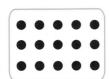

1. **Do these sets have more than, fewer than or the same amount as the set above? Tick the correct answer.**

more than ☐   less than ☐   the same as ☐

more than ☐   less than ☐   the same as ☐

more than ☐   less than ☐   the same as ☐

more than ☐   less than ☐   the same as ☐

more than ☐   less than ☐   the same as ☐

more than ☐   less than ☐   the same as ☐

Recap
- I know if one set has more or less than another. ○ ○ ○
- I can work out how many more than or less than there are in a set. ○ ○ ○

1. Freddie Frog wants to see his family. Help him by writing the missing numbers on the lily pads.

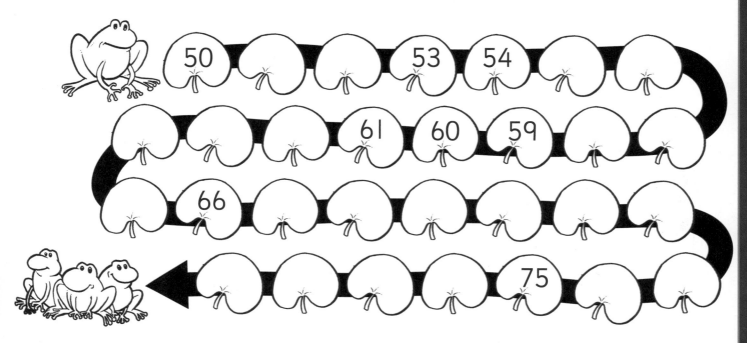

2. Fill in the missing numbers.

41	42	43		45		47		49	50
51		53	54		56		58		60
	62			65		67		69	
71		73	74		76		78		80

| fifty |
| sixty |
| seventy |
| eighty |

3. Trace over the numbers and words

50 fifty   60 sixty

70 seventy   80 eighty

Finished Early? Colour the lily pads with even numbers green.

Strand: Number
Curriculum Objectives:
Count the number of objects in a set;
read, write and order numerals, 0–99.

Counting to 100

1. **Freda Fairy wants to reach the sparkling star. Help her by writing the missing numbers on the flowers.**

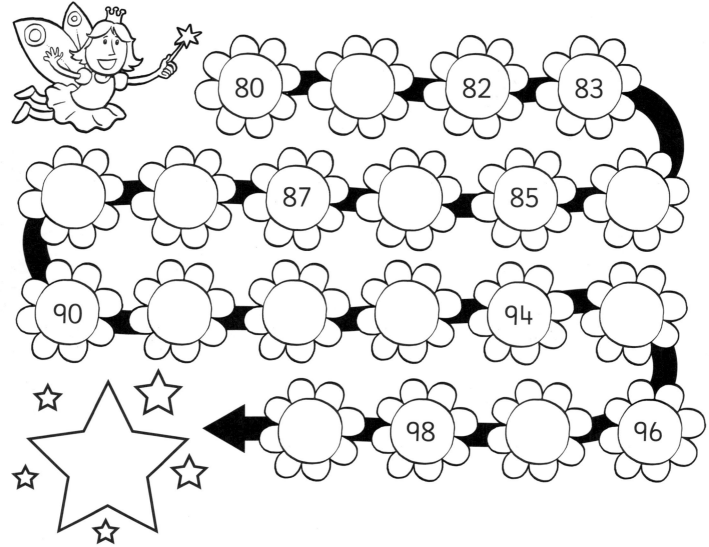

2. **Fill in the missing numbers.**

71	72			75		77	78		80	eighty
81		83		85	86		88			ninety
	92		94	95		97		99	100	one hundred

Finished Early?
Colour the flowers with odd numbers red.

Rows and Columns

column

1	2	3	4	5	6	7	8	9	10
11	12	13	14	15	16	17	18	19	20
21	22	23	24	25	26	27	28	29	30
31	32	33	34	35	36	37	38	39	40
41	42	43	44	45	46	47	48	49	50
51	52	53	54	55	56	57	58	59	60
61	62	63	64	65	66	67	68	69	70
71	72	73	74	75	76	77	78	79	80
81	82	83	84	85	86	87	88	89	90
91	92	93	94	95	96	97	98	99	100

row

1. **What's missing in these columns?**

1	6	
11	16	18
21		28
		38
51		58
	66	
71	76	78
91	96	

2. **Write the missing numbers from these rows.**

31	32			35	36				40
71		73	74			77		79	
	42	43					48		50
		93		95		97		99	

Using a 100-Square

1	2	3	4	5	6	7	8	9	10
11	12	13	14	15	16	17	18	19	20
21	22	23	24	25	26	27	28	29	30
31	32	33	34	35	36	37	38	39	40
41	42	43	44	45	46	47	48	49	50
51	52	53	54	55	56	57	58	59	60
61	62	63	64	65	66	67	68	69	70
71	72	73	74	75	76	77	78	79	80
81	82	83	84	85	86	87	88	89	90
91	92	93	94	95	96	97	98	99	100

When you want to find a number on the 100-square, look at the number in the units place.
If you want to find 65, go down the 5 column
If someone says the number, listen for the last part.
If you want to find 27, go down the 7 column.

1. **Colour the following numbers in the hundred square:**

   71   32   13   95   46   88   59   60

2.

1	2	🍎	4	5	6	7	8	9	10		🍎 =	3
11	12	13	14	15	🍊	17	18	19	20		🍊 =	
21	22	23	24	25	26	27	28	🍌	30		🍌 =	
🍐	32	33	34	35	36	37	38	39	40		🍐 =	
41	42	43	44	🍒	46	47	48	49	50		🍒 =	
51	52	53	54	55	56	57	🍓	59	60		🍓 =	
61	62	63	64	65	66	67	68	69	🍓		🍓 =	
71	72	73	74	75	76	🫐	78	79	80		🫐 =	
81	🍇	83	84	85	86	87	88	89	90		🍇 =	
91	92	93	🍋	95	96	97	98	99	100		🍋 =	

Recap

- I can read, write and order numbers to 100. ○ ○ ○

19. The 100-Square

1. **Fill in the missing numbers.**

1		3			6			9	
	12			15			18		
21		23				27			30
	32				36			39	
	42			45			48		
51			54		56				60
		63				67		69	
	72			75			78		
81					86				90
		93				97			100

2. **Look at these 100-square puzzles. Fill in the missing pieces.**

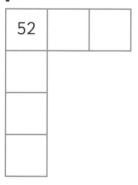

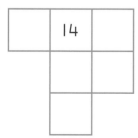

100-Square

1	2	3	4	5	6	7	8	9	10
11	12	13	14	15	16	17	18	19	20
21	22	23	24	25	26	27	28	29	30
31	32	33	34	35	36	37	38	39	40
41	42	43	44	45	46	47	48	49	50
51	52	53	54	55	56	57	58	59	60
61	62	63	64	65	66	67	68	69	70
71	72	73	74	75	76	77	78	79	80
81	82	83	84	85	86	87	88	89	90
91	92	93	94	95	96	97	98	99	100

Start at 7. Jump on 8 spaces. You land on 15.

$7 + 8 =$?

1. $11 + 9 =$ ☐ $23 + 7 =$ ☐ $47 + 11 =$ ☐

2. $12 + 2 =$ ☐ $78 + 5 =$ ☐ $81 + 3 =$ ☐

3. $34 + 9 =$ ☐ $43 + 6 =$ ☐ $64 + 8 =$ ☐

4. $71 + 6 =$ ☐ $70 + 7 =$ ☐ $53 + 8 =$ ☐

5. **Start on 15 and jump 9 spaces. You land on** ☐

6. **Start on 42 and jump 7 spaces. You land on** ☐

7. **Start on 82 and jump 8 spaces. You land on** ☐

8. **On your 100-square put an X through these answers:**

   a) 10 more than 40
   b) 10 less than 42
   c) 10 more than 51
   d) 10 less than 67

Finished Early?
Circle on the 100-square:
- 20 more than 50
- 30 more than 70
- 20 less than 60

100-Square

1	2	3	4	5	6	7	8	9	10
11	12	13	14	15	16	17	18	19	20
21	22	23	24	25	26	27	28	29	30
31	32	33	34	35	36	37	38	39	40
41	42	43	44	45	46	47	48	49	50
51	52	53	54	55	56	57	58	59	60
61	62	63	64	65	66	67	68	69	70
71	72	73	74	75	76	77	78	79	80
81	82	83	84	85	86	87	88	89	90
91	92	93	94	95	96	97	98	99	100

Colour Code your 100-Square!

Use your 100-square and your crayons to help you with these activities:

1. Circle all the numbers with 3 in the units place.
2. Colour all the numbers with 2 in the tens place red.
3. Colour all the numbers with 9 in the units place green.
4. Colour all the numbers with 4 in the tens place blue.
5. Colour all the numbers with 6 in the units place brown.
6. Colour all the numbers with 5 in the tens place purple.

Recap
- I can add numbers using the 100-square.
- I can recognise number patterns.
- I can work out number patterns.

20. Subtraction 2

Another way of saying 'subtract' is asking 'How many more than?'

Tim has 8 sweets. Leah has 5. How many more sweets than Leah does Tim have?

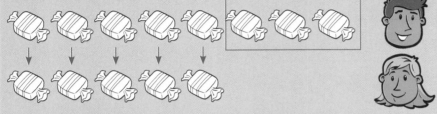

8 – 5 = 3 Tim has 3 more sweets than Leah.

1. **Mark had 9 lollipops. Tom had 6. How many more did Mark have?**

 Mark: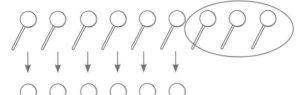

 Tom:

9 – 6 = ☐ Mark had ☐ more lollipops than Tom.

2. **Leon had 6 tractors. Susie had 5 tractors. How many more tractors did Leon have?**

 Leon: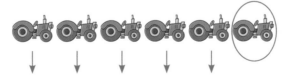

 Susie:

☐ – ☐ = ☐ Leon has ☐ more than Susan.

Strand: Number
Curriculum Objectives:
Develop an understanding of subtraction as deducting, as complementing and as difference 0–20;
develop and/or recall mental strategies for subtraction 0–20;
construct number sentences and number stories;
solve problems involving subtraction 0–20;
estimate differences within 99;
subtract numbers without renaming within 99;
use the symbols +, –, =;
solve one-step problems involving addition or subtraction.

| 1 | 2 | 3 | 4 | 5 | 6 | 7 | 8 | 9 | 10 | 11 | 12 | 13 | 14 | 15 | 16 | 17 | 18 | 19 | 20 |

I had 17 apples. I ate 6. How many had I left?
Start at 17. Make the kangaroo jump 6 spaces back. He lands on 11.
So 17 − 6 = 11

1. **James had 19 tractors. He sold 7. How many had he left?** 19 − 7 = ☐

2. **Clare had 16 dolls. She gave 8 to her sister. How many dolls had she left?** 16 − 8 = ☐

3. **Tom had 20 cars. He gave 9 of them to Liam. How many had he left?** 20 − 9 = ☐

4. **Sarah had 15 teddies. She gave 8 to Shane. How many had she left?** 15 − 8 = ☐

5. **Carmel had 12 books. She read 6. How many books had she left to read?** 12 − 6 = ☐

6. **Cara had 20 apples. She gave 10 to Bobby. How many had she left?** 20 − 10 = ☐

7. **Now try these:**

14	19	18	17	10	16	18
− 7	− 6	− 9	− 6	− 5	− 4	− 5
☐	☐	☐	☐	☐	☐	☐

Subtracting Tens and Units

Use your lollipop sticks to help you.

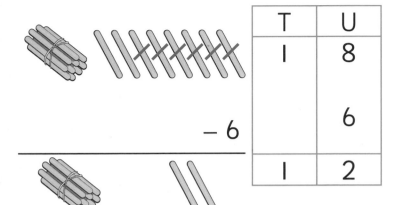

T	U
1	8
	6
1	2

$- 6$

💡 **Remember your tens and units rule:**
Work out the **units** first and then work out the **tens**.

1.

t	u
1	5
−	3

t	u
1	6
−	2

t	u
1	4
−	3

t	u
1	9
−	6

t	u
1	8
−	3

t	u
1	7
−	2

t	u
1	9
−	5

2.

t	u
1	3
−	9

t	u
1	7
−	1

t	u
1	8
−	7

t	u
1	7
−	6

t	u
1	8
−	8

t	u
1	7
−	5

3.

t	u
2	9
−	8

t	u
4	7
−	9

t	u
1	9
−	2

t	u
1	6
−	4

t	u
1	7
−	6

t	u
3	8
−	6

Recap

- I know how to subtract bigger numbers.
- I can subtract numbers with tens and units in them.

○ ○ ○
○ ○ ○

21. Addition 5

Count the lollipop sticks. Write the sum.

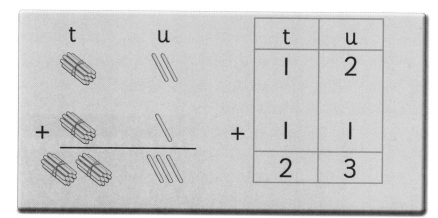

t	u
1	2
1	1
2	3

1.

t	u
1	4
2	1
3	5

2.

t	u
1	5
	4
1	9

3.

t	u
2	3
1	1

4.

t	u

5.

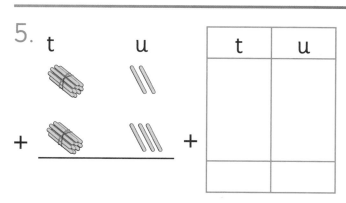

t	u

6.

t	u

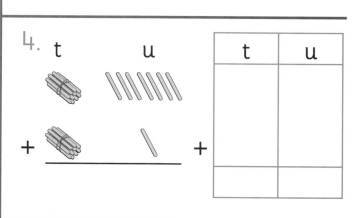

Strand: Number

Curriculum Objectives:
Develop an understanding of addition by combining;
add numbers without renaming within 99.

Count the lollipop sticks. Write the sum.

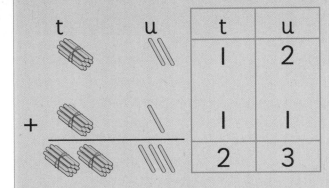

t	u
1	2
1	1
2	3

t	u
4	4
3	1
7	5

Count the units and the tens. Write the answer.

1.

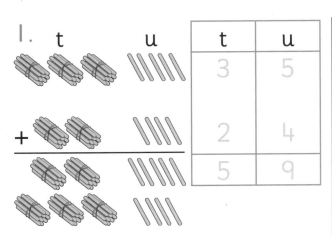

t	u
3	5
2	4
5	9

2.

t	u
2	3
5	1

3.

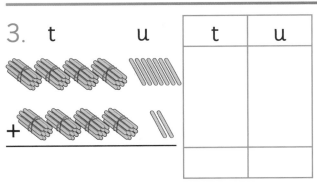

t	u

4.

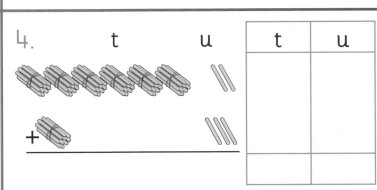

t	u

5.

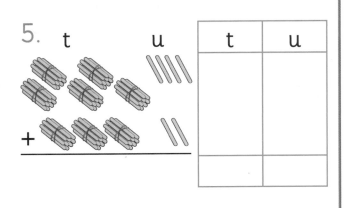

t	u

6.

t	u

Place the tens and units on the board.
Put the units together and then put the tens together to find
the answer.

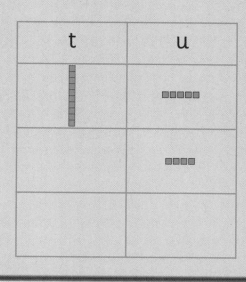

```
t u
1 5
+  4
```

```
t u
1 5
+  4
1 9
```

1. **Place your tens and units on the board.**

```
t u
1 6
+  3
```

t	u

```
t u
2 5
+1 2
```

t	u

```
t u
  4
+2 1
```

t	u

```
t u
1 3
+2 5
```

t	u

2.
```
t u
2 1
+2 4
```
□
```
t u
  1
+4 4
```
□
```
t u
2 4
+1 5
```
□
```
t u
1 7
+3 2
```
□
```
t u
1 5
+3 3
```
□
```
t u
1 2
+3 6
```
□
```
t u
2 0
+3 0
```
□
```
t u
3 3
+  6
```
□

Place the tens and units on the board.
Put the units together and then put the tens together to find the answer.

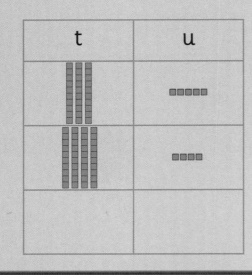

```
  t u              t            u
  3 5
+ 4 4
```

```
  t u              t            u
  3 5
+ 4 4
  7 9
```

Use your notation board. Add the units first.

1.
```
 t u    t u    t u    t u    t u    t u    t u    t u
 6 8    5 2    2 8    7 6    4 1    2 2    6 0    4 3
+2 1   +1 3   +3 1   +2 2   +3 3   +6 5   +3 9   +2 6
[  ]   [  ]   [  ]   [  ]   [  ]   [  ]   [  ]   [  ]
```

2.
```
 t u    t u    t u    t u    t u    t u    t u    t u
 2 1    5 1    8 4    1 7    1 0    1 2    5 0    9 1
+5 5   +4 4   +1 5   +4 2   +8 3   +7 6   +3 0   +  6
[  ]   [  ]   [  ]   [  ]   [  ]   [  ]   [  ]   [  ]
```

3.
```
 t u    t u    t u    t u    t u    t u    t u    t u
 2 8    5 7    8 1    1 1    1 5    1 1    6 5    1 9
+5 1   +2 2   +  7   +4 8   +7 3   +8 8   +2 0   +8 0
[  ]   [  ]   [  ]   [  ]   [  ]   [  ]   [  ]   [  ]
```

```
 t u    First place 1 ten and 4 units on the board.
 1 4    Then put 2 tens and 1 unit on the board.
+2 1    Count the units. Write down the answer.
        Count the tens. Write down the answer.
```

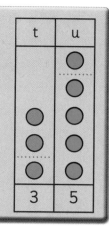

1.
t u	t u	t u	t u
5 0	7 1	2 4	3 1
+1 6	+2 4	+1 1	+1 8

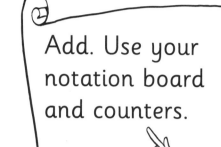

Add. Use your notation board and counters.

2.
t u	t u	t u	t u
4 1	2 2	6 5	1 0
+4 4	+3 1	+1 2	+3 0

3.
t u	t u	t u	t u	t u	t u
5 2	5 0	7 1	2 4	3 1	8 4
+2 7	+1 6	+1 4	+1 1	+1 8	+1 5

4. **Try these without your cubes. Add the units first.**

t u	t u	t u	t u	t u	t u	t u	t u
7 2	1 1	6 2	5 6	7 2	2 4	8 1	2 3
+1 6	+2 7	+2 7	+1 3	+2 4	+5 5	+1 5	+1 5

22. Check-up 2

| 1 | 2 | 3 | 4 | 5 | 6 | 7 | 8 | 9 | 10 | 11 | 12 | 13 | 14 | 15 | 16 | 17 | 18 | 19 | 20 |

1. 10 − 2 = ☐   9 − 3 = ☐   4 − 2 = ☐   5 − 1 = ☐

2. a) John had 8 sweets. He gave 3 to Alan. How many had he
   left? 8 − 3 = ☐

   b) Charlie had 7 grapes. His dog ate 5.
   How many were left? ☐ − ☐ = ☐

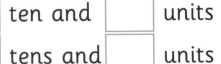

3. **Put in the missing numbers.**

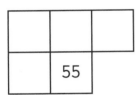
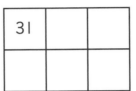
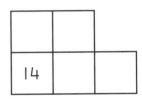

4. **How many tens and units?**

   12 = ☐ ten and ☐ units   17 = ☐ ten and ☐ units

   32 = ☐ tens and ☐ units   27 = ☐ tens and ☐ units

5.
```
 t u        t u        t u        t u        t u        t u
 1 6        1 9        1 8        1 9        1 8        1 7
- 5        - 9        - 7       -1 2        - 6        - 8
[  ]       [  ]       [  ]       [  ]       [  ]       [  ]
```

6.
```
 t u        t u        t u        t u        t u        t u
 2 4        5 2        1 2        7 1        1 4        3 5
+1 3       +1 7       +1 2       +2 4       +1 1       +2 3
[  ]       [  ]       [  ]       [  ]       [  ]       [  ]
```

Curriculum Objective:
To revise concepts that were explored in units 16-21.

23. Money 1

How much altogether?

1.  = ☐ c

2.  = ☐ c

3.  = ☐ c

4.  = ☐ c

5.  = ☐ c

6.  = ☐ c

7.  = ☐ c

8. = ☐ c

9.  = ☐ c

10. = ☐ c

Finished Early?
Make some rubbings of these coins.

Strand: Measures
Curriculum Objectives:
Recognise, exchange and use coins up to the value of 50 cents;
calculate and give change;
calculate how many items can be bought with a given sum.

How much altogether?

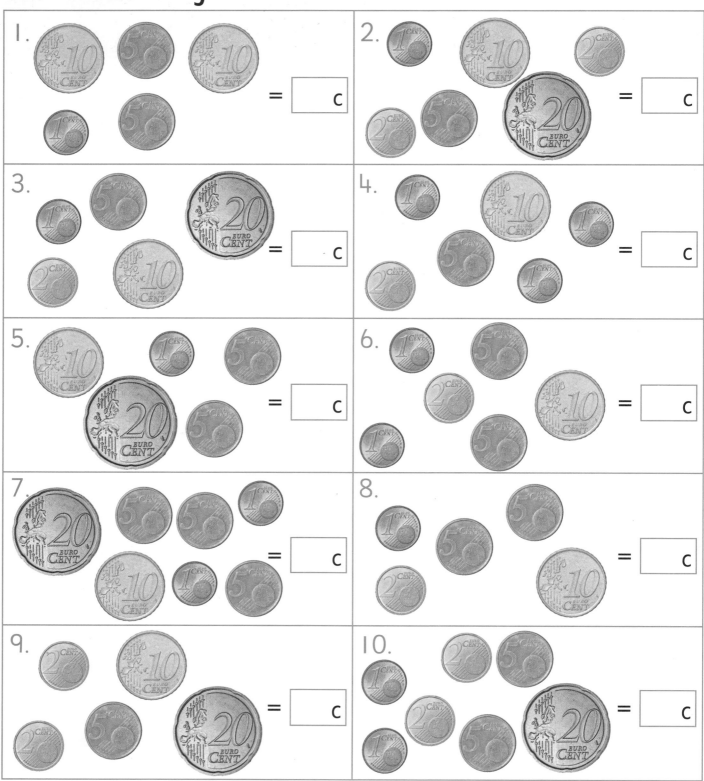

1. = ☐ c

2. = ☐ c

3. = ☐ c

4. = ☐ c

5. = ☐ c

6. = ☐ c

7. = ☐ c

8. = ☐ c

9. = ☐ c

10. = ☐ c

Puzzler
Milly has 5 coins in her piggy bank. She has 3 gold coins and 2 bronze coins. What is the largest and smallest total she could have in her piggy bank?

1. **What coins do you need?**

7c =	9c = 
11c =	15c = 
19c = 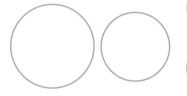	13c = 
22c = 	27c = 
34c = 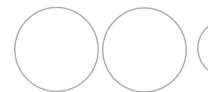	36c = 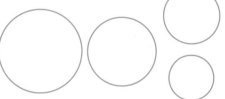
45c = 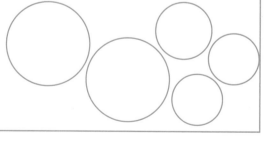	49c = 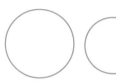

2. **Make 48c in two different ways.**

48c =	48c =

At the Toy Shop

book	teddy	ball	doll	boat	kite

7c   10c   8c   9c   5c   14c

1. **How much is it for a book** **and a boat** **?**

   7c + 5c = 12c

2. **How much is it for a teddy** **and a ball** **?**

   ☐ + ☐ = ☐

3. **How much is it for a kite** **and a boat** **?**

   ☐ + ☐ = ☐

4. **How much is it for a book** **a ball** **and a boat** ☐ **?**

   ☐ + ☐ + ☐ = ☐

5. **How much more money does the kite**  **cost than the book** ☐ **?**

   ☐ − ☐ = ☐

6. **I have 5c. How much more do I need to buy the kite** ☐ **?** ☐

7. **Jack has 15c. He buys a teddy** **and a boat** **.**

   Has he enough money? | Yes | | No |

   Does he get change? | Yes | | No |

   💡 Colour the correct box.

Change from 20 Cents

The apple cost 13c and you have 20c. How much change will you get? Count on to get the change.

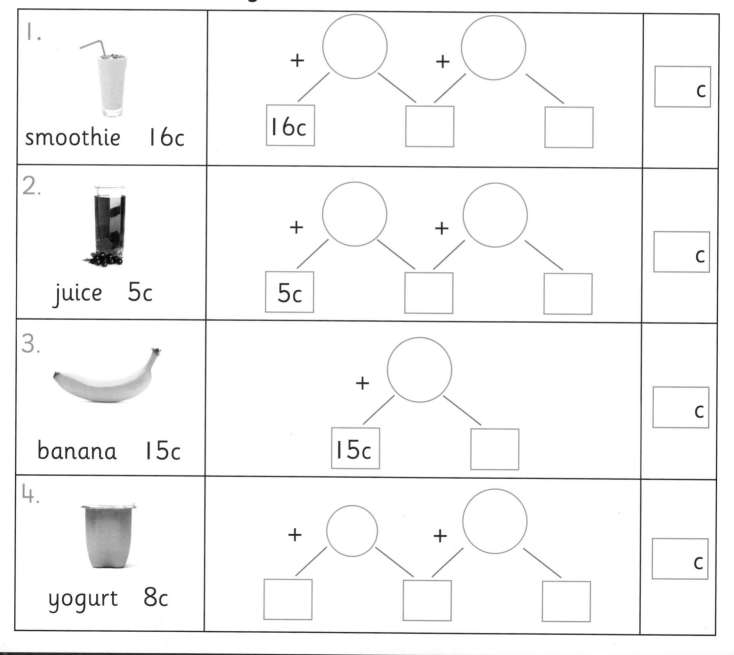

13c   + 13c   + 15c   20c   change: 7c

The change is 2c and 5c. That makes 7c altogether.

Now find the change from 20c:

1.	smoothie 16c	+ ◯ + ◯ 16c ▢ ▢	▢ c
2.	juice 5c	+ ◯ + ◯ 5c ▢ ▢	▢ c
3.	banana 15c	+ ◯ 15c ▢	▢ c
4.	yogurt 8c	+ ◯ + ◯ ▢ ▢ ▢	▢ c

24. Length

1. Colour the longer object in each pair.

a)   b)   c)

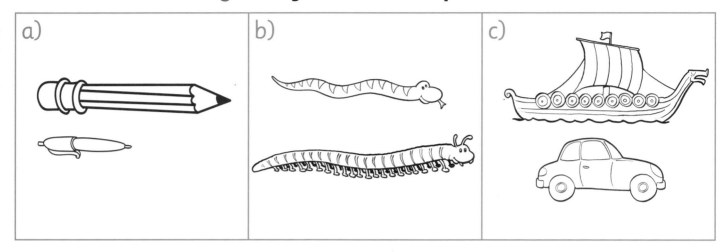

2. Colour the taller object in each pair.

a)   b)   c)

3. Colour the longer object in each pair.

a)   b)   c)

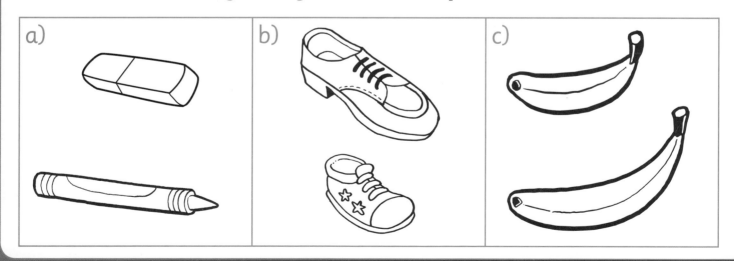

Strand: Measures
Curriculum Objectives:
Estimate, compare, measure and record length using non-standard units;
select and use appropriate non-standard measuring units and instruments;
estimate, measure and record length using standard unit (the metre);
solve and complete practical tasks and problems involving length.

1. **Circle the shorter object in each pair.**
2. **Colour the taller animal in box e) blue and colour the shorter animal red.**

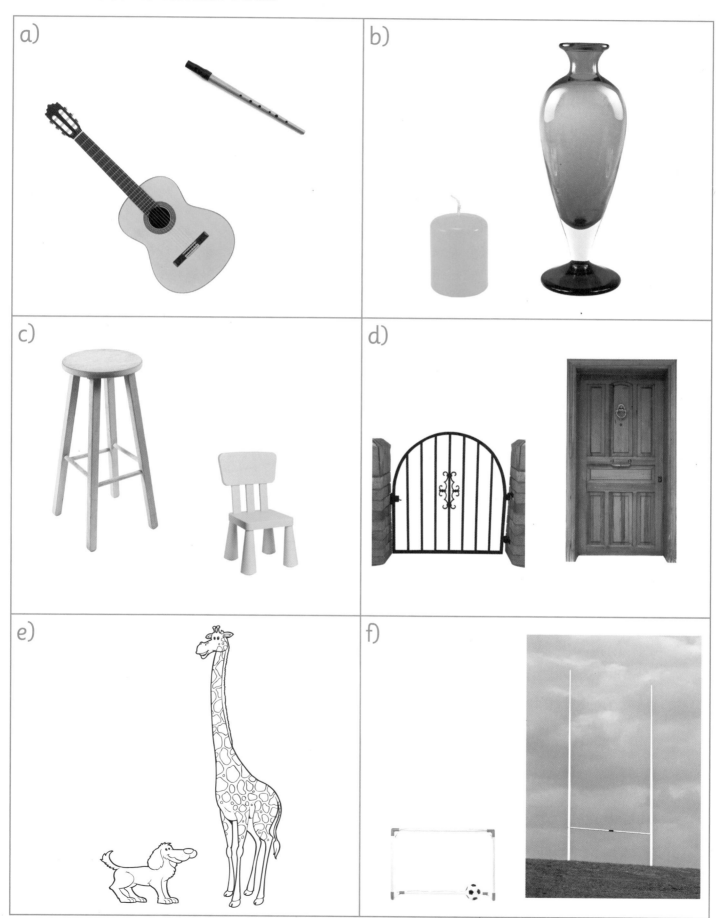

a)

b)

c)

d)

e)

f)

Draw and Colour

1.		**Draw a longer scarf.**
2.		**Draw a shorter tree.**
3.		**Draw a wider house.**
4.		**Draw a narrower road.**

5. **Colour the longest**	
6. **Colour the tallest**	
7. **Colour the widest**	
8. **Colour the narrowest**	

Measuring

1. **Estimate, then measure the length and width of your table. Use:**

unit	estimate	length	estimate	width

2. **With your partner, use your stride to measure:**

	estimate	measure
length of the classroom		
width of the classroom		
length of the playground		
width of the playground		

a) Did you and your partner get the same answer? _____

b) Why/why not?_____

One Metre

1 metre

| 0 | 10 | 20 | 30 | 40 | 50 | 60 | 70 | 80 | 90 | 100 |

cm

(*not to scale)

1. **Estimate then check using a metre stick ✓ your estimate below.**

object	about a metre	shorter than a metre	longer than a metre

Recap
- I know how long a metre is.
- I can use a metre stick.

888

What Is a Half?

1. Colour half of each shape.

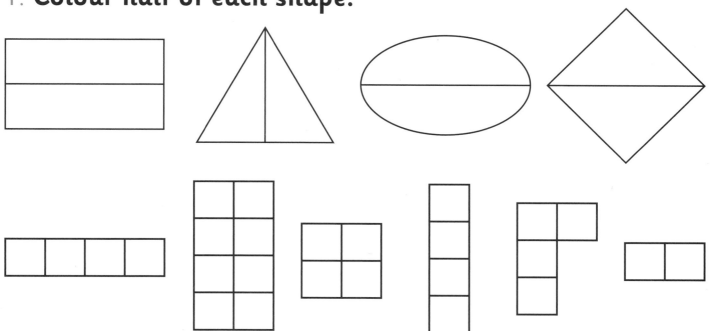

2. Colour the shapes that show two halves.

Strand: Number
Curriculum Objective:
Establish and identify halves of sets up to 20.

103

1. **Colour half of each set.**

2. Colour half of each set.

$\frac{1}{2}$ of 8 = ☐

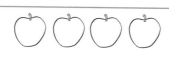

$\frac{1}{2}$ of 12 = ☐

$\frac{1}{2}$ of 10 = ☐

$\frac{1}{2}$ of 4 = ☐

$\frac{1}{2}$ of 16 = ☐

$\frac{1}{2}$ of 6 = ☐

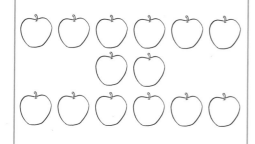

$\frac{1}{2}$ of 14 = ☐

$\frac{1}{2}$ of 2 = ☐

$\frac{1}{2}$ of 20 = ☐

3. $\frac{1}{2}$ of 10 = ☐ $\frac{1}{2}$ of 4 = ☐ $\frac{1}{2}$ of 18 = ☐

$\frac{1}{2}$ of 6 = ☐ $\frac{1}{2}$ of 14 = ☐ $\frac{1}{2}$ of 12 = ☐

$\frac{1}{2}$ of 8 = ☐ $\frac{1}{2}$ of 16 = ☐ $\frac{1}{2}$ of 20 = ☐

1. **Draw the other half.**

Recap
- I know how to colour half of a shape.
- I can find half of a set.
- I can draw the other half of a shape.

26. Place Value 2

Write the number.

1. a) 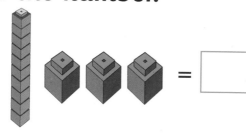 = ☐   b) 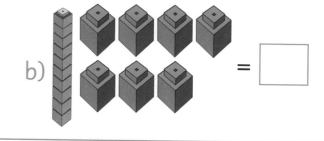 = ☐

2. a) 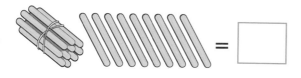 = ☐   b)  = ☐

3. a) [image] = ☐   b) [image] = ☐

4. a) [image] = ☐   b) [image] = ☐

5. a) [image] = ☐   b) 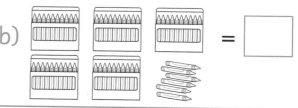 = ☐

6. a) 12 = ☐ ten ☐ units   7. a) 54 = ☐ tens ☐ units

   b) 18 = ☐ ten ☐ units   b) 36 = ☐ tens ☐ units

   c) 16 = ☐ ten ☐ units   c) 28 = ☐ tens ☐ units

   d) 19 = ☐ ten ☐ units   d) 7 = ☐ tens ☐ units

   e) 11 = ☐ ten ☐ unit   e) 72 = ☐ tens ☐ units

   f) 17 = ☐ ten ☐ units   f) 80 = ☐ tens ☐ units

Strand: Number

Curriculum Objective:
Explore, identify and record place value 0–99.

107

We can show tens and units on an abacus. Look at the abacus below and find the number each abacus shows.

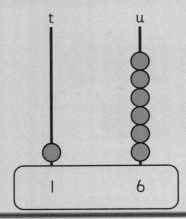

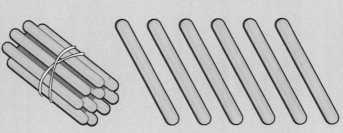

16 = 1 ten + 6 units

1.

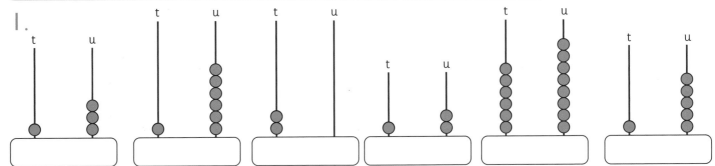

We can also show tens and units on notation boards.

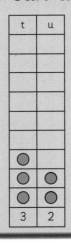

32 = 3 tens + 2 units

2.

t	u		t	u		t	u		t	u		t	u		t	u

1. **Show these numbers on the abacus.**

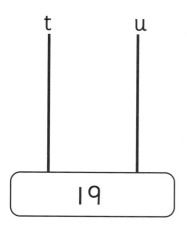
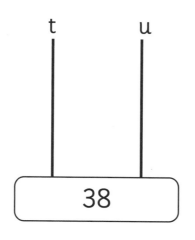
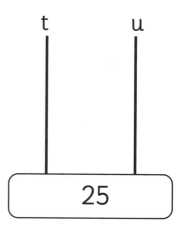

19   38   25

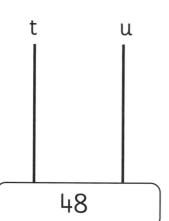
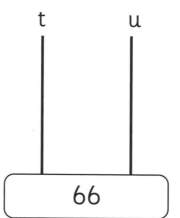
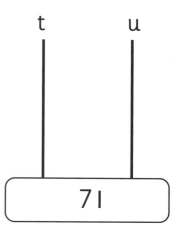

48   66   71

2. **Show these numbers on the notation board.**

t	u		t	u		t	u		t	u		t	u		t	u
1	9		3	8		2	5		4	8		6	6		7	1

Finished Early?
Draw notation boards to show these numbers in your copy. 21   34   16   40   53

Groups of Tens

What happens when we have groups of tens? We can count in tens!

t   t

2 groups of tens = 20.

1. **Now find out what numbers these make:**

t t t   t t t t   t t t t t   t t t t t t t   t t   t t t t t t

☐ ☐ ☐ ☐ ☐ ☐

2. **Match each of these with the right number:**

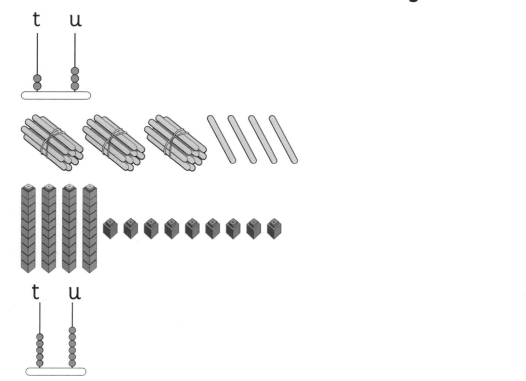

49

56

23

34

3. **Now try these:**

18 = ☐ ten and ☐ units   3 tens and 3 units = ☐

25 = ☐ tens and ☐ units   4 tens and 1 unit   = ☐

11 = ☐ ten and ☐ unit   1 ten and 2 units   = ☐

37 = ☐ tens and ☐ units   7 tens and 4 units = ☐

58 = ☐ tens and ☐ units   2 tens and 9 units = ☐

46 = ☐ tens and ☐ units   8 tens and 4 units = ☐

62 = ☐ tens and ☐ units   5 tens and 7 units = ☐

19 = ☐ ten and ☐ units   6 tens and 8 units = ☐

10 = ☐ ten and ☐ units   2 tens and 0 units = ☐

29 = ☐ tens and ☐ units   7 tens and 7 units = ☐

4. **Colour the balloons that make 18.**

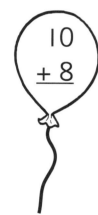

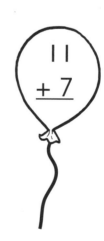
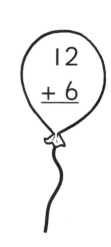

| 10 +8 | 9 +9 | 8 +7 | 9 +8 | 11 +7 | 12 +6 |

5. **Colour the balloons that make 19.**

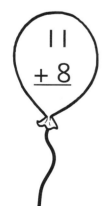
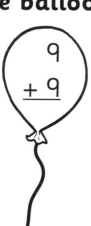

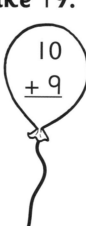
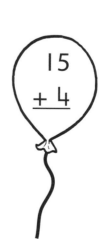

| 11 +8 | 9 +9 | 12 +7 | 10 +9 | 15 +4 | 6 +8 |

1. **Show tens and units on the abacus**

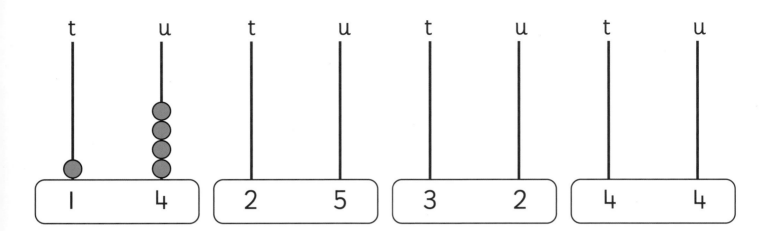

t	u
1	4

t	u
2	5

t	u
3	2

t	u
4	4

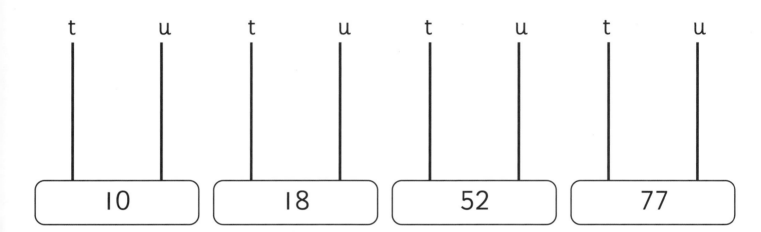

t	u
10	

t	u
18	

t	u
52	

t	u
77	

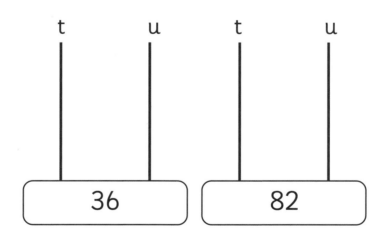

t	u
36	

t	u
82	

2. **Circle the 'ten' in each number, e.g. ②4.**

13   45   64   39   27   86   19   22   5

59   47   97   30   52   38   64   70   60

Crack the Code!

Write the units in this number	35 =	☐	→ e
Write the tens in this number	47 =	☐	→ a
Write the units in this number	72 =	☐	→ l
Write the tens in this number	61 =	☐	→ h
Write the units in this number	11 =	☐	→ p
Write the tens in this number	80 =	☐	→ t
Write the units in this number	19 =	☐	→ n

5	2	5	1	6	4	9	8

1. **Draw a picture of what you discover here.**

Tens and Units

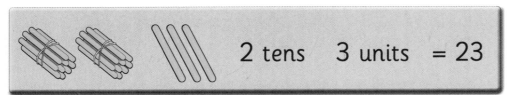

2 tens   3 units   = 23

1. Write the numbers.

☐ tens ☐ units	☐ tens ☐ units	☐ tens ☐ units
☐ tens ☐ units	☐ tens ☐ unit	☐ tens ☐ units
☐ tens ☐ units	☐ tens ☐ units	☐ tens ☐ units
☐ tens ☐ units	☐ tens ☐ units	☐ tens ☐ units

Recap
- I know the place value of numbers up to 99
- I can count in tens.
- I can show a number on an abacus and on a notation board.

27. Subtraction 3

Subtracting Tens

1. **Use the 100-square to work these out:**

30 – 10 = ☐   50 – 10 = ☐   70 – 10 = ☐

40 – 20 = ☐   60 – 30 = ☐   80 – 20 = ☐

90 – 40 = ☐   70 – 50 = ☐   60 – 10 = ☐

20 – 10 = ☐   40 – 30 = ☐   80 – 50 = ☐

50 – 20 = ☐   60 – 40 = ☐   100 – 60 = ☐

2. **Now try these:**

90	100	30	60	80	50
– 20	– 70	– 30	– 20	– 30	– 30

70	60	100
– 60	– 50	– 50

90	80	60
– 60	– 40	– 60

90	80	100
– 10	– 30	– 70

1	2	3	4	5	6	7	8	9	10
11	12	13	14	15	16	17	18	19	20
21	22	23	24	25	26	27	28	29	30
31	32	33	34	35	36	37	38	39	40
41	42	43	44	45	46	47	48	49	50
51	52	53	54	55	56	57	58	59	60
61	62	63	64	65	66	67	68	69	70
71	72	73	74	75	76	77	78	79	80
81	82	83	84	85	86	87	88	89	90
91	92	93	94	95	96	97	98	99	100

Strand: Number
Curriculum Objectives:
Develop an understanding of subtraction as deducting, as complementing and as difference 0–20;
develop and/or recall mental strategies for subtraction 0–20;
estimate differences within 99;
subtract numbers without renaming within 99;
use the symbols +, –, =;
solve one-step problems involving addition or subtraction.

115

3. **Use a 100-square to answer these.**

a) John had 60 sweets. He gave 30 to Eric. How many sweets had he left? 60 – 30 = ☐

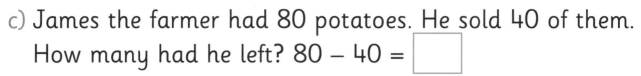

b) Ciara had 70 marbles. She lost 20 of them. How many had she left? 70 – 20 = ☐

c) James the farmer had 80 potatoes. He sold 40 of them. How many had he left? 80 – 40 = ☐

d) There were 90 ants on the wall. 50 of them ran under a pot. How many were left on the wall? 90 – 50 = ☐

e) There were 40 grapes on a vine. 30 of them fell off. How many were left on the vine? 40 – 30 = ☐

f) There were 30 birds on a wire. 10 flew away. How many were left? 30 – 10 = ☐

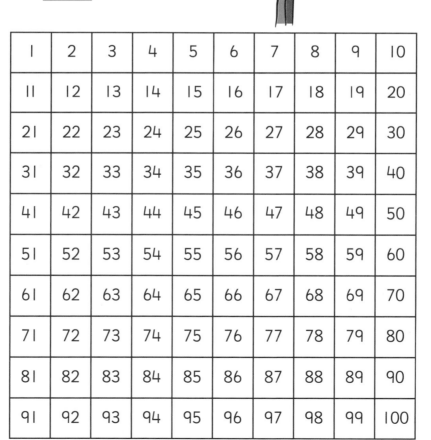

1	2	3	4	5	6	7	8	9	10
11	12	13	14	15	16	17	18	19	20
21	22	23	24	25	26	27	28	29	30
31	32	33	34	35	36	37	38	39	40
41	42	43	44	45	46	47	48	49	50
51	52	53	54	55	56	57	58	59	60
61	62	63	64	65	66	67	68	69	70
71	72	73	74	75	76	77	78	79	80
81	82	83	84	85	86	87	88	89	90
91	92	93	94	95	96	97	98	99	100

Crack the Code!

When you have cracked the code, draw what you find!

t u	t u	t u	t u	t u
7	1 9	7 0	1 9	7
− 3	− 4	−2 0	− 8	− 4
____ = T	____ = P	____ = W	____ = G	____ = K

t u	t u	t u	t u	t u
9 0	1 6	9	1 8	1 3
−3 0	−1 0	− 2	−1 3	−1 1
____ = O	____ = U	____ = I	____ = E	____ = S

t u	t u	t u	t u	t u	t u
8 0	1 6	1 7	5 0	2 0	4 0
−4 0	− 6	− 4	−2 0	− 3	−2 0
____ = L	____ = A	____ = Y	____ = N	____ = H	____ = R

4	50	60

15	6	15	15	7	5	2

15	40	10	13	7	30	11

7	30

4	17	5

15	10	20	3

1. Try these using notation boards.

```
  t u              t u              t u
  4 6              7 6              4 4
 -2 4             -4 5             -2 3
 ____             ____             ____
```

```
  t u              t u              t u
  6 9              3 8              4 3
 -1 4             -1 5             -2 2
 ____             ____             ____
```

2.

```
  t u        t u        t u        t u        t u        t u        t u
  3 8        2 9        8 8        5 4        6 8        5 4        6 5
 -1 4       -1 5       -3 6       -3 1       -4 7       -3 2       -4 2
 ____       ____       ____       ____       ____       ____       ____
```

```
  t u        t u        t u        t u        t u        t u        t u
  5 6        3 9        6 5        5 3        3 7        5 4        9 6
 -3 4       -2 5       -1 4       -3 1       -1 7       -5 3       -6 2
 ____       ____       ____       ____       ____       ____       ____
```

```
  t u        t u        t u        t u        t u        t u        t u
  5 5        3 3        7 6        9 4        8 5        5 9        4 7
 -2 4       -2 1       -5 6       -8 2       -3 5       -3 2       -3 7
 ____       ____       ____       ____       ____       ____       ____
```

Recap

- I can subtract tens.
- I can solve word problems using subtraction.
- I can subtract using a notation board.

28. 3-D Shapes

Here are some 3-D shapes. 3-D shapes are not flat.

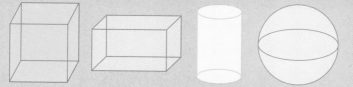

This is a square, which is a 2-D shape ☐. It is flat.

This is a cube, which is a 3-D shape ☐. It is not flat.

1. **Match each 3-D shape with the correct object.**

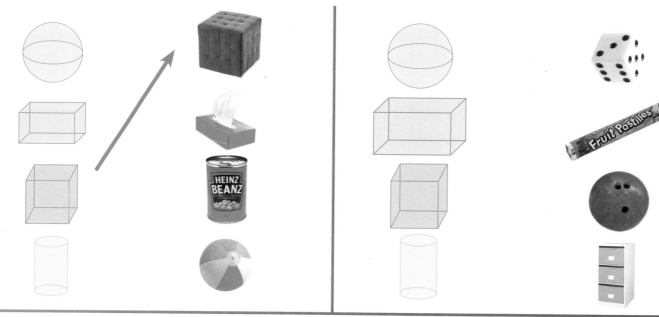

2. **How many?**

cubes ☐

cuboids ☐

cylinders ☐

spheres ☐

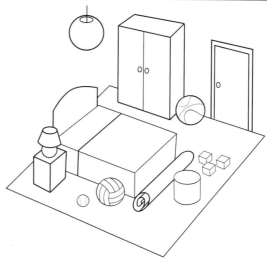

Strand: Shape and Space
Curriculum Objectives:
Describe, compare and name 3-D shapes, including cube, cuboid, cylinder and sphere;

discuss the use of 3-D shapes in the environment;
solve and complete practical tasks and problems involving 2-D and 3-D shapes;
explore the relationship between 2-D and 3-D shapes.

1. **Set up a slope. Check if these shapes roll or slide.** ✓

shape		rolls	slides
cube			
cuboid			
sphere			
cylinder			

2. **Use your 3-D shapes to help you. Colour the correct answer.**

   a) Can you stack cubes?   Yes   No

   b) Can you stack cuboids?   Yes   No

   c) Can you stack cylinders?   Yes   No

   d) Can you stack spheres?   Yes   No

3. **Use your 3-D shapes to build:**

   a) a house b) a flagpole c) a ball pool d) a truck

   Talk about the shapes you used.

Game Time

Play I Spy in the classroom. 'I spy with my little eye something in the shape of . . .' a cube, a cuboid, etc.

Puzzler

Can you build a cube, cuboid or cylinder using lollipop sticks?

More About 3-D Shapes

3-D shapes have faces, corners and edges.

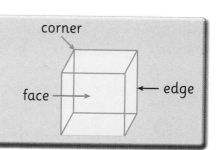

1. **Fill in the table below.**

shape	faces	edges	corners
cube			
cuboid			
cylinder			
sphere			

2. **What 3-D shapes can you see?**

3. **In your copy draw the faces of these 3-D shapes.**
   What 2-D shapes will you find? You could trace around your 3-D shapes to help you.

Recap
- I can recognise and name these 3-D shapes – cube, cuboid, sphere and cylinder.
- I know how many faces, edges and corners there are on these 3-D shapes.
- I know which of them can slide, roll and stack.

29. Ordinal Numbers

1st first   2nd second   3rd third   4th fourth   5th fifth   6th sixth   7th seventh   8th eighth   9th ninth   10th tenth

The Big Boat Race

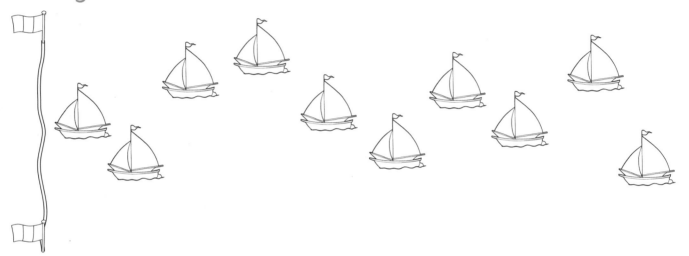

1. **Can you do these?**
   a) Colour the first boat red.
   b) Draw a square around the second boat.
   c) Colour the third boat yellow.
   d) Draw a circle around the fourth boat.
   e) Colour the fifth boat green.
   f) Draw a triangle around the sixth boat.
   g) Colour the seventh boat blue.
   h) Draw a rectangle around the eighth boat.
   i) Colour the ninth boat pink.
   j) Draw a purple star around the tenth boat.

2. **What colour is the last boat?**

Strand: Number
Curriculum Objectives:
Use the language of ordinal number, first to tenth.

1st	2nd	3rd	4th	5th	6th	7th	8th	9th	10th
first	second	third	fourth	fifth	sixth	seventh	eighth	ninth	tenth

Leah

Mark

Josh

Lucy

Kate

Susie

Elsa

John

Me

Welcome to my apartment block!

- No one lives on the ground floor.
- I live on the first floor.
- Look carefully and see where my friends live.

1. **Which floor does Mark live on? The** [ ] **floor.**

2. **Which floor does Kate live on? The** [ ] **floor.**

3. **Does Lucy live on the fifth floor? Yes or No?** [ ]

4. **A girl lives on the ninth floor. True or False?** [ ]

5. **Who lives on the fourth floor?** [ ]

6. **Who lives on the seventh floor?** [ ]

7. **Which floor does Elsa live on? The** [ ] **floor.**

8. **John lives on the floor above me.**
   Which floor is that? The [ ] **floor.**

9. **Who lives on the ninth floor?** [ ]

Puzzler

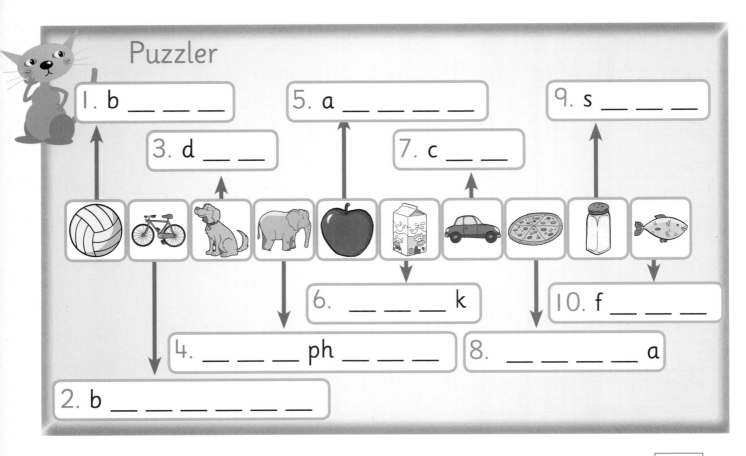

1. b _ _ _

3. d _ _

5. a _ _ _ _

7. c _ _ _

9. s _ _ _

6. _ _ _ k

10. f _ _ _

4. _ _ _ ph _ _ _

8. _ _ _ _ a

2. b _ _ _ _ _ _ _

1. a) Go to the FIRST word. What is the FOURTH letter? ☐

   b) Go to the SEVENTH word. What is the SECOND letter? ☐

   c) Go to the EIGHTH word. What is the THIRD letter? ☐

   d) Go to the SECOND word, what is the FOURTH letter? ☐

   e) The **third** letter of the **first** word is ☐

   f) The **second** letter of the **last** word is ☐

   g) The **fourth** letter of the **eighth** word is ☐

   h) The **second** letter of the **ninth** word is ☐

   i) The **third** letter of the **seventh** word is ☐

   j) The **first** letter of the **third** word is ☐

Draw the character

Recap
• I understand the order of things: first to tenth. ◯ ◯ ◯

30. Check-up 3

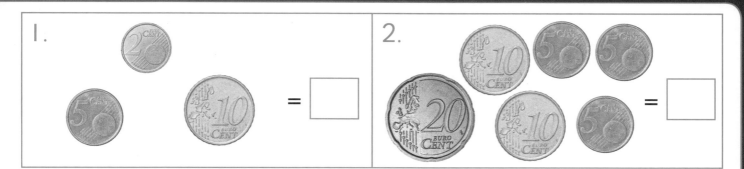

1. [coins] = ☐

2. [coins] = ☐

3. 11c = ◯ ◯

4. 34c = ◯ ◯ ◯ ◯

5. **Draw.**

shorter than a metre	about a metre	longer than a metre

6. $\frac{1}{2}$ of 4 = ☐ $\frac{1}{2}$ of 20 = ☐ $\frac{1}{2}$ of 12 = ☐ $\frac{1}{2}$ of 18 = ☐

7. 23 = ☐ tens and ☐ units.   ☐ = 5 tens and 6 units.

8.
```
 t u       t u       t u       t u       t u       t u       t u
 3 7       5 8       2 9       4 9       1 9       6 2       5 8
-1 1      -3 5      -1 2      -2 4      -  3      -3 1      -1 2
─────     ─────     ─────     ─────     ─────     ─────     ─────
```

9. **Fill in the table.**

shape	how many faces?	how many edges?	how many corners?
cube [image]			
cylinder [image]			

Curriculum Objective:
To revise concepts that were explored in units 23-29.

31. 100-Square Subtraction

1	2	3	4	5	6	7	8	9	10
11	12	13	14	15	16	17	18	19	20
21	22	23	24	25	26	27	28	29	30
31	32	33	34	35	36	37	38	39	40
41	42	43	44	45	46	47	48	49	50
51	52	53	54	55	56	57	58	59	60
61	62	63	64	65	66	67	68	69	70
71	72	73	74	75	76	77	78	79	80
81	82	83	84	85	86	87	88	89	90
91	92	93	94	95	96	97	98	99	100

$25 - 7 = \boxed{?}$

Start on 25. Jump **back** 7 spaces. You land on 18.
So $25 - 7 = 18$.

1. $15 - 9 = \boxed{}$ $36 - 5 = \boxed{}$ $47 - 10 = \boxed{}$ $58 - 3 = \boxed{}$

   $12 - 7 = \boxed{}$ $78 - 5 = \boxed{}$ $18 - 3 = \boxed{}$ $70 - 7 = \boxed{}$

   $28 - 6 = \boxed{}$ $34 - 9 = \boxed{}$ $64 - 8 = \boxed{}$ $53 - 8 = \boxed{}$

2. a) Start on 35. Jump **back** 9 spaces. You land on $\boxed{}$.

   b) Start on 46. Jump **back** 7 spaces. You land on $\boxed{}$.

   c) Start on 82. Jump **back** 6 spaces. You land on $\boxed{}$.

   d) Start on 50. Jump **back** 6 spaces. You land on $\boxed{}$.

Finished Early?
Colour the answers on the 100-square:

- 20 **less** than 50   • 30 **less** than 70   • 40 **less** than 60

Strand: Number
Curriculum Objectives:
Develop an understanding of subtraction as deducting, as complementing and as difference 0–20;
develop and/or recall mental strategies for subtraction 0–20;

construct number sentences and number stories;
estimate differences within 99;
subtract numbers without renaming within 99;
use the symbols +, −, =;
solve one-step problems involving addition or subtraction.

100-Square

1	2	3	4	5	6	7	8	9	10
11	12	13	14	15	16	17	18	19	20
21	22	23	24	25	26	27	28	29	30
31	32	33	34	35	36	37	38	39	40
41	42	43	44	45	46	47	48	49	50
51	52	53	54	55	56	57	58	59	60
61	62	63	64	65	66	67	68	69	70
71	72	73	74	75	76	77	78	79	80
81	82	83	84	85	86	87	88	89	90
91	92	93	94	95	96	97	98	99	100

1. **Use your crayons to help you do the following:**
   a) Colour all the numbers with 5 in the units place red.
   b) Colour all the numbers with 0 in the tens place yellow.
   c) Colour all the numbers with 2 in the units place green.
   d) Colour all the numbers with 8 in the tens place brown.
   e) Colour all the numbers with 6 in the tens place orange.

2. **Write the missing numerals.**

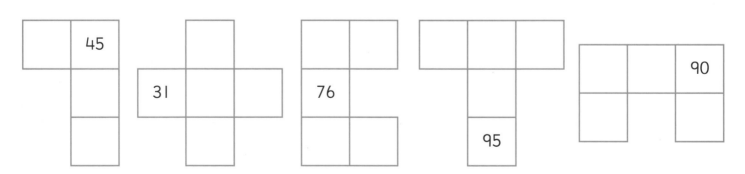

More Subtraction using the 100-Square

1	2	3	4	5	6	7	8	9	10
11	12	13	14	15	16	17	18	19	20
21	22	23	24	25	26	27	28	29	30
31	32	33	34	35	36	37	38	39	40
41	42	43	44	45	46	47	48	49	50
51	52	53	54	55	56	57	58	59	60
61	62	63	64	65	66	67	68	69	70
71	72	73	74	75	76	77	78	79	80
81	82	83	84	85	86	87	88	89	90
91	92	93	94	95	96	97	98	99	100

Remember to jump back on the 100-square

1. 16 − 8 = ☐
2. 28 − 9 = ☐
3. 30 − 10 = ☐
4. 45 − 8 = ☐
5. 22 − 3 = ☐
6. 61 − 9 = ☐
7. 60 − 10 = ☐
8. 33 − 7 = ☐

25 − 5 = ☐
11 − 6 = ☐
34 − 9 = ☐
52 − 7 = ☐
54 − 5 = ☐
73 − 7 = ☐
44 − 8 = ☐
57 − 10 = ☐

19 − 4 = ☐
17 − 10 = ☐
29 − 8 = ☐
68 − 10 = ☐
86 − 7 = ☐
85 − 4 = ☐
51 − 5 = ☐
28 − 4 = ☐

Recap
- I know how to use the 100-square to subtract. ○ ○ ○
- I can recognise number patterns on the 100-square. ○ ○ ○

32. Time 2

This is a clock. It has two hands.
One hand is long. One hand is short.
It has 12 numbers. The short hand is at 7.
The long hand is at 12.
This clock says 7 o'clock.

1. **In pairs, find out how you know when the clock says:**
   9 o'clock   11 o'clock   5 o'clock   12 o'clock   2 o'clock

2. **Make the clocks say the times in Megan's diary.**

Megan's diary			
breakfast	7 o'clock	singing	1 o'clock
school	9 o'clock	art	2 o'clock
reading	10 o'clock	home time	3 o'clock
break time	11 o'clock	bedtime	8 o'clock

Strand: Measures
Curriculum Objectives:
Use the vocabulary of time to sequence events;
read and record time using simple devices;
read time in hours and half-hours on 12-hour analogue clock;
read day, date and month using calendar.

129

Half Past

half past	$\frac{1}{2}$ past

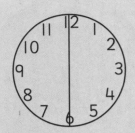

This clock is in two parts

Each part is called a half

The long hand is at 6

It shows half past — $\frac{1}{2}$ past

This clock says $\frac{1}{2}$ past 7

1. **Write the time under the clock.**

☐ past ☐   ☐ past ☐   ☐ past ☐   ☐ past ☐

2. **Make the clocks say:**

half past 3 $\frac{1}{2}$ past 8   half past 12 $\frac{1}{2}$ past 4

Finished Early?

In your copy draw clocks to show these times.

$\frac{1}{2}$ past 9 $\frac{1}{2}$ past 2 $\frac{1}{2}$ past 11 $\frac{1}{2}$ past 4

Children's Channel

1 o'clock	Pony Club	
$\frac{1}{2}$ past 1	Cartoons	
2 o'clock	All about Dogs	
$\frac{1}{2}$ past 2	Cook with Captain Cook	
3 o'clock	Art with Andy	
$\frac{1}{2}$ past 3	Dancing with Dee Dee	

1. **What time does *All about Dogs* start?** _____

2. **What time do the cartoons begin?** _____

3. **When does *Dancing with Dee Dee* begin?** _____

4. **What time does *Art with Andy* finish?** _____

5. **What is on television at $\frac{1}{2}$ past 2?** _____

Finished Early?
In your copy write a simple timetable for your day.

Recap
- I can read the time on a clock.   ◯ ◯ ◯
- I can draw a clock that shows time in hours and half hours   ◯ ◯ ◯
- I can read a simple timetable.   ◯ ◯ ◯

33. Addition 6

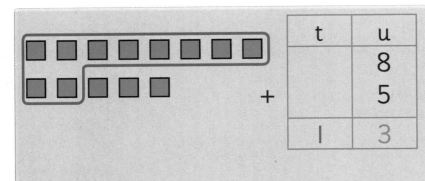

t	u
	8
+	5
1	3

To add 8 + 5, ring 10 cubes to make a ten. Write 1 in the tens column. There are 3 cubes left over. Write 3 in the units column.

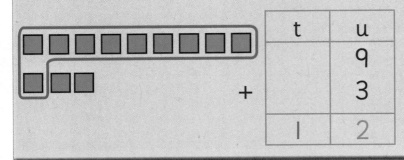

t	u
	9
+	3
1	2

To add 9 + 3, ring 10 cubes to make a ten. Write 1 in the tens column. Write 2 in the units column.

Ring ten cubes to make a bundle of ten.

1.

t	u
	6
+	9

2.

t	u
	7
+	9

3.

t	u
	8
+	8

4.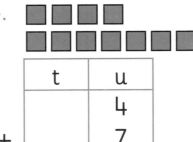

t	u
	4
+	7

Strand: Number
Curriculum Objectives:
Develop an understanding of addition by combining or partitioning sets, use concrete materials 0–20; explore, develop and apply the commutative, associative and zero properties of addition;

develop and/or recall mental strategies for addition facts within 20; construct number sentences and number stories; solve problems involving addition within 20; add numbers without and with renaming within 99; explore and discuss repeated addition and group counting.

Addition

Add 16 + 5. Place the tens and units on a notation board.

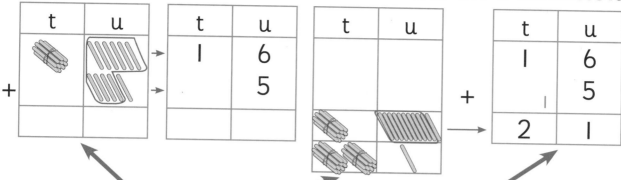

First add the units: 6 + 5. You will get 11. Make a bundle of ten. Place it in the tens column.

Place the 1 unit in the units answer box. Then add the tens: 1 + 1 = 2. Place the 2 tens in the tens answer box.

1.

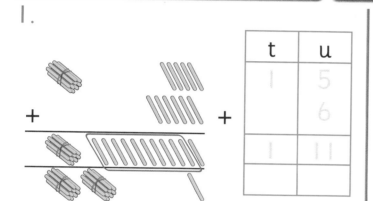

t	u
1	5
	6
1	11

2.

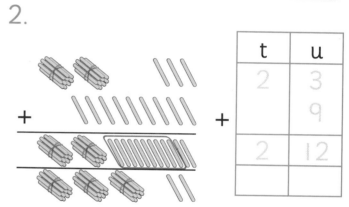

t	u
2	3
	9
2	12

3.

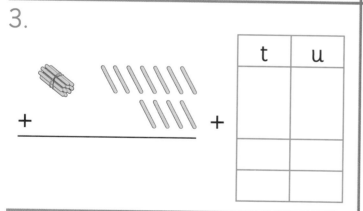

t	u

4.

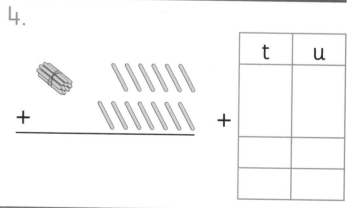

t	u

5.

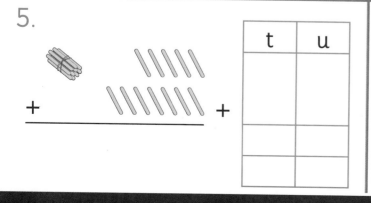

t	u

6.

t	u

Place the tens and units on the board.

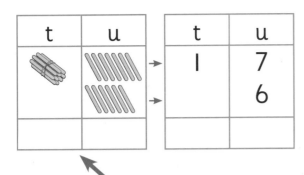

t	u
I	7
	6

t	u

t	u
I	7
+	6
2	3

Add the units first. Check to see if you can make a ten, if so place the ten in the tens column.

Place any left over units in the units answer box. Then add the tens and place the answer in the tens column.

1.

+ _____ +

t	u

2.

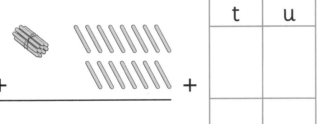

+ _____ +

t	u

3.

t	u
I	4
	9
+	

4.

t	u
I	6
	8
+	

5.

t	u
I	2
	9
+	

6.

t	u
I	5
	8
+	

7.

t	u
I	9
	3
+	

8.

t	u
I	4
	8
+	

1. Use your notation board to add these sums.

t u	t u	t u	t u	t u	t u
1 8	1 2	1 8	1 6	2 5	2 9
+ 6	+1 9	+1 7	+2 6	+1 8	+1 5

2.

t u	t u	t u	t u	t u	t u
2 8	3 7	2 4	4 7	1 5	5 8
+1 6	+2 8	+ 8	+3 9	+3 8	+1 8

3.

t u	t u	t u	t u	t u	t u
1 7	1 8	1 6	2 3	2 5	2 7
+1 6	+1 8	+2 9	+2 8	+2 5	+1 7

4.

t u	t u	t u	t u	t u	t u
1 7	3 3	2 9	3 8	3 9	3 7
+2 9	+1 9	+4 9	+4 3	+1 4	+2 9

We can do addition sums in a quicker way.

t	u
2	6
1 ,	5
4	1

+

6 + 5 = 11

11 = 1 ten and 1 unit

Put 1 in the unit column and the 1 ten in the ten column.

Add all the tens 2 + 1 + 1 = 4

Your answer is 4 tens and 1 unit = 41

1. **Use your notation board to add these sums.**

t u	t u	t u	t u	t u	t u	t u
1 6	2 7	1 8	2 9	1 5	3 5	2 5
+¹ 8	+ 9	+ 8	+ 4	+ 9	+ 6	+ 8
2 4						

2.

t u	t u	t u	t u	t u	t u	t u
1 6	2 7	1 8	2 9	1 5	3 5	2 5
+1 9	+1 7	+3 6	+1 5	+1 5	+1 8	+2 9

3.

t u	t u	t u	t u	t u	t u	t u
1 7	2 4	2 3	3 7	1 2	3 3	2 4
+1 5	+2 9	+3 8	+2 4	+4 9	+1 7	+4 8

4.

t u	t u	t u	t u	t u	t u	t u
2 4	1 9	3 8	2 9	4 7	2 6	1 7
+1 6	+ 7	+ 4	+1 7	+ 6	+2 6	+1 7

Estimate

Look at the tens first and put a ring around your estimate.
Add and check your estimate.

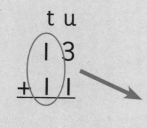

```
 t u
 1 3
+1 1
```

10 + 10 = 20.
My estimate is 20.

```
 t u
 1 3
+1 1
 2 4
```

My estimate was 20 and the answer was 24.

1.
a)
```
 t u
 1 2
+1 4
 2 6
```
20
30

b)
```
 t u
 1 1
+2 3
```
30
20

c)
```
 t u
 2 1
+1 4
```
20
30

d)
```
 t u
 2 2
+1 5
```
40
30

e)
```
 t u
 1 3
+3 4
```
30
40

f)
```
 t u
 2 1
+2 5
```
30
40

g)
```
 t u
 1 3
+2 0
```
30
20

h)
```
 t u
 2 2
+2 3
```
50
40

i)
```
 t u
 3 1
+2 3
```
60
50

j)
```
 t u
 3 0
+1 4
```
30
40

k)
```
 t u
 2 0
+4 4
```
60
50

l)
```
 t u
 5 2
+1 0
```
60
70

m)
```
 t u
 4 1
+4 1
```
90
80

n)
```
 t u
 3 5
+4 1
```
70
60

o)
```
 t u
 7 9
+2 0
```
80
90

1.

	t u
	2 3
+	1 8
	4 1

	t u
	2 6
+	1 9

	t u
	1 5
+	3 8

	t u
	2 7
+	2 4

	t u
	1 5
+	5 6

	t u
	2 4
+	3 7

2.

	t u
	1 7
+	1 5

	t u
	2 3
+	2 9

	t u
	2 3
+	3 7

	t u
	3 7
+	2 4

	t u
	1 2
+	4 9

Recap
· I can add numbers without and with renaming within 99.

○ ○ ○

1. a) Draw a man **between** the two planes.
   b) Draw a ball **underneath** the blue lorry.
   c) Draw a flag **on top of** the tower.
   d) Draw a skipping rope **around** the suitcase.
   e) Draw a dog to the **left** of the blue lorry.
   f) Draw a bird flying to the **right** of the tower.
   g) Draw the sun peeping **through** the clouds.

Strand: Shape and Space

Curriculum Objectives:
Explore, discuss and develop and use the vocabulary of
spatial relations – between, underneath, on top of, around,
through, left and right.

139

35. Subtraction 4

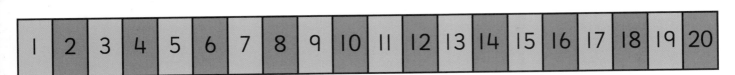

| 1 | 2 | 3 | 4 | 5 | 6 | 7 | 8 | 9 | 10 | 11 | 12 | 13 | 14 | 15 | 16 | 17 | 18 | 19 | 20 |

Number Stories

1. **Mary had 20 sweets. She gave 9 of them to her friend Jess. How many had she left?** $20 - 9 = \boxed{11}$

2. **John had 14 pieces of Lego. 7 of the pieces were broken. How many pieces were not broken?**

   $\boxed{} - \boxed{} = \boxed{}$

3. **Mammy bought 19 packets of crisps for Sam's birthday party. 15 children were at the party. How many packets of crisps were left over?** $\boxed{} - \boxed{} = \boxed{}$

4. **Matthew was playing golf. He had 14 golf balls. He lost 5 of them. How many golf balls had he left?**

   $\boxed{} - \boxed{} = \boxed{}$

5. **Tom has 17 toy cars. He can only find 13. How many are missing?** $\boxed{} - \boxed{} = \boxed{}$

6. **Mammy planted 18 flowers. 7 did not grow. How many flowers grew?** $\boxed{} - \boxed{} = \boxed{}$

Strand: Number
Curriculum Objectives:
Develop an understanding of subtraction as deducting, as complementing and as difference 0–20;
develop and/or recall mental strategies for subtraction 0–20;
construct number sentences and number stories;
estimate differences within 99;
subtract numbers without renaming within 99;
use the symbols +, -, =;
solve one-step problems involving addition or subtraction.

Subtraction

1. **There are 27 children in Jack's class. There are 14 girls. How many boys are in Jack's class?**

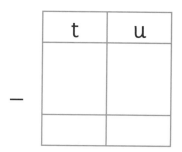

2. **Mary went to Spain for 59 days. It rained for 16 days. How many days were sunny?**

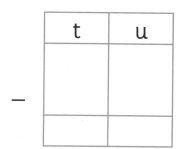

3. **Jessica had 46 dolls. Her sister broke 13 of her dolls. How many dolls were left?**

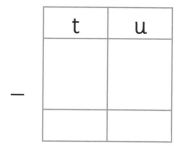

4. **Pat counted 77 animals at the zoo. 23 animals were in the water. How many were not in the water?**

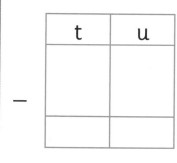

Recap
- I know how to solve subtraction word problems.

○ ○ ○

36. Money 2

1. How much altogether?

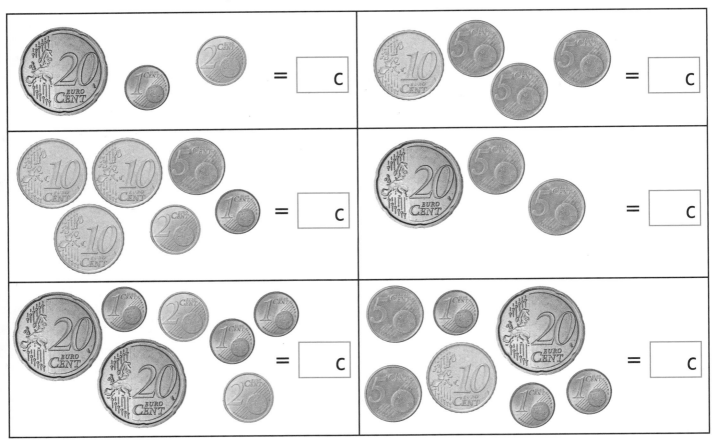

2. What coins do you need?

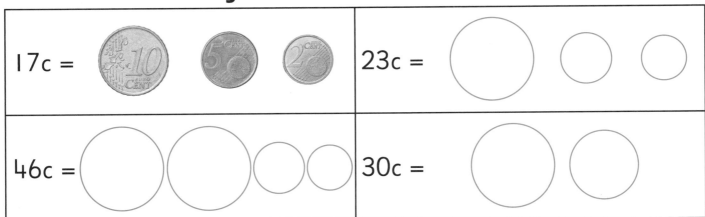

Strand: Measures
Curriculum Objectives:
To recognise, exchange and use coins up to the value of 50 cent;
to calculate and give change;
to calculate how many items may be bought with a given sum.

Change from 50c

The doll costs 46c and you have 50c. How much change will you get? Count on to get the change.

$+$ → 46c → 48c → 50c

change = 4c

The change is 2c and 2c. This makes 4c altogether.

change

1.  44c skipping rope	$+$ 1c → 44c → 45c, $+$ 5c → 50c	= ☐ c
2. 35c hula hoop	$+$ ◯ → ☐ c → ☐ c, $+$ ◯ → ☐ c	= ☐ c
3.  25c stickers	$+$ ◯ → ☐ c → ☐ c, $+$ ◯ → ☐ c	= ☐ c
4. 38c jigsaw	$+$ ◯ → ☐ c → ☐ c, $+$ ◯ → ☐ c	= ☐ c

Ita's Ice Cream Van   Fabulous Flavours!

chocolate
20c

mint
15c

strawberry
25c

vanilla
15c

1. **Mammy wants a mint ice cream** and **Anna wants a chocolate one** .

   How much must they pay altogether? [ ] c

2. **Daddy wants a vanilla ice-cream** and **Peter wants a strawberry one** .

   How much must they pay altogether? [ ] c

3. **Granny wants to buy two chocolate ice-creams** .

   How much does she pay altogether? [ ] c

4. **Which ice cream costs the same as the vanilla one** ?

   _____

5. **How many chocolate ice-creams** **can you get for 50c?** [ ] c

6. **Jim bought a strawberry ice-cream** .
   What change did he get from 50c? [ ] c

Recap
- I know these coins.
- I can add coins to 50c.
- I can swap coins to 50c.
- I can find the cost of items and get the change from 50c.

37. Capacity

1. **How many egg cups does it takes to fill each container?**

object	my estimate	my measurement
bowl		
plastic cup		
jug		
yoghurt pot		

2. **Which container holds the most?**

3. **Which container holds the least?**

4. **Would you use an egg cup or a plastic cup to fill the bucket?**

Why?

Strand: Measures
Curriculum Objectives:
Estimate, compare, measure and record capacity using non-standard units;

select and use appropriate non-standard measuring units and instruments;
estimate, measure and record capacity using standard unit (the litre) and solve simple problems.

145

How many egg cups does each container hold?

1. Which container holds the most?
2. Which container holds the least?
3. How many egg cups fill the yoghurt pot?
4. How many egg cups fill the glass?
5. How many egg cups would fill 2 cans?
6. How many more egg cups does it take to fill the glass than the can?
7. How many egg cups would it take to fill 2 yoghurt pots and 1 can?
8. Does the glass hold more than or less than a yoghurt pot?
9. Two yoghurt pots hold more than one glass. True or false?

1 Litre

1. **Draw the containers into the correct boxes.**

holds more than a litre (l)	holds less than a litre (l)

2. **How many**  **can be filled from a litre bottle? Estimate first, then measure.**

container	my estimate	my measurement

At Home

Find containers. Draw one that holds 1 litre, one that holds less than a litre and one that holds more than a litre.

holds 1 litre (1l)	holds less than a litre (l)	holds more than a litre (l)

True or False? ✓ or ✗

1. **I will find the word 'litre' on:**

   a) a bottle of cola ☐   b) a box of cornflakes ☐

   c) a carton of milk ☐

2. **A cup can hold 1 litre of milk.** ☐

3. **Mammy can buy 1 litre of petrol.** ☐

4. **A litre carton of milk looks the same as a litre bottle of water.** ☐

5. **I can buy a litre of bananas.** ☐

Recap
• I know what the word **capacity** means. ◯ ◯ ◯
• I can estimate and measure a litre using different containers. ◯ ◯ ◯

38. Addition 7

Counting in Twos

1. **Colour the numbers that Joey landed on.**
   He is hopping in twos.

| 0 | 1 | 2 | 3 | 4 | 5 | 6 | 7 | 8 | 9 | 10 | 11 | 12 | 13 | 14 | 15 | 16 | 17 | 18 | 19 | 20 |

Joey landed on

2. **How many socks? Count in twos.**

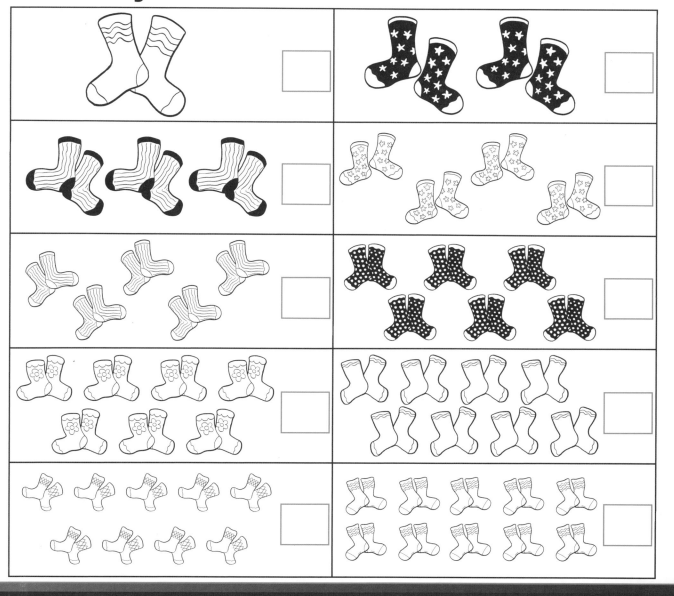

Strand: Number
Curriculum Objectives:
Develop and/or recall mental strategies for addition
facts within 20;

explore and discuss repeated addition and
group counting.

149

Counting in Fives

The grasshopper jumps in fives.

1. **Colour the numbers he stops on.**

1	2	3	4	5	6	7	8	9	10
11	12	13	14	15	16	17	18	19	20
21	22	23	24	25	26	27	28	29	30
31	32	33	34	35	36	37	38	39	40
41	42	43	44	45	46	47	48	49	50

2. **The grasshopper stopped on:**

5									

3. **How many leaves? Count in fives.**

a) = ☐ leaves

b) = ☐ leaves

c) = ☐ leaves

4. **Lead the dog to the bone by counting in fives. Colour.**

28	1	22	34	9	33	50
11	36	2	16	43	40	45
27	19	44	30	35	8	32
7	37	20	25	3	21	13
26	15	46	12	41	23	42
47	10	17	6	31	4	39
5	18	29	38	14	48	24

Counting in Tens

1.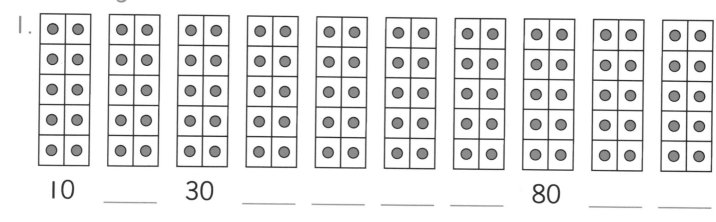

10 _____ 30 _____ _____ _____ 80 _____ _____

2. **How many toes?**

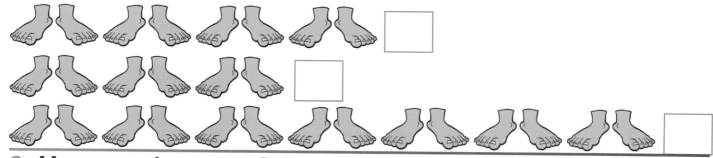

3. **How much money?**

c

c

4. **Count in tens and colour the path to the bone.**

10	1	22	34	9	33	50
20	30	2	16	43	40	45
27	40	44	30	35	8	32
7	37	50	25	3	21	13
26	15	46	60	70	23	42
47	10	17	6	31	80	39
5	18	29	38	14	90	100

Recap

• I know how to count in twos, fives and tens. ○ ○ ○

39. Weight

1. **Are these objects heavier or lighter than your school bag? Estimate, and ✓.**

object	heavier	lighter

2. **How many cubes balance the fruit? Estimate first, then measure.**

object	my estimate	how many cubes?

Strand: Measures
Curriculum Objectives:
Estimate, compare, measure and record weight using non-standard units;

select and use appropriate non-standard measuring units and instruments;
estimate, measure and record weight using standard unit (the kilogram) and solve simple problems.

Weight

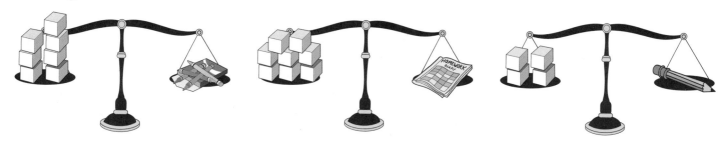

1. a) How many cubes balance the crayons? ☐

   b) How many cubes balance the pencil? ☐

   c) Which item is the lightest? _____

   d) Which item is the heaviest? _____

   e) Would 2 boxes of crayons be heavier than 1 journal?

   Yes ☐ / No ☐

   f) How many cubes would you need to balance 2 boxes of crayons? ☐

2. **Use cubes to measure the weight of these items.**

item		weight
book		
rubber		
ruler		
pencil case		

heavier	**lighter**

a) The pencil case is _____ than the ruler.

b) The rubber is _____ than the book.

c) The book is _____ than the ruler.

One Kilogram (1kg)

All of these things weigh 1 kilogram (1kg).

1. **Are the objects in the table heavier, lighter or about the same as 1kg?** ✓

object	heavier	lighter	about the same
(lunchbox)			
(school bag)			
(chair)			
(pencil case)			

2. **Estimate, then measure how many of each object you will need to make 1kg. Use a scale and a 1kg weight.**

object	estimate	weight	difference
(orange)			
(apple)			
(marbles)			

potatoes	flour	coal	oranges
1 kg	3 kg	5 kg	2 kg

1. **Which bag is the heaviest?** _____
   How much does it weigh? ⬚ kg

2. **Which bag is the lightest?** _____
   How much does it weigh? ⬚ kg

3. **Put the bags in order, starting with the lightest:**

   a) Bag of _____   b) Bag of _____

   c) Bag of _____   d) Bag of _____

4. **Which is heavier: 3 bags of potatoes or 1 bag of coal?** _____

5. **Which is lighter: 2 bags of potatoes or 1 bag of flour?** _____

6. **Ella bought 2 bags of oranges and 1 bag of potatoes. What did they weigh?** ⬚ kg

Recap
- I can use a balance.
- I can estimate and measure the weight of objects.
- I know a kilogram is used to measure weight.

○ ○ ○

○ ○ ○

40. Check-up 4

1. 26 - 10 = ☐   35 - 15 = ☐   49 - 13 = ☐

2.   t u   t u   t u
     1 5   2 4   1 9
    +1 6   +   8   +2 3
    ‾‾‾‾‾‾   ‾‾‾‾‾‾   ‾‾‾‾‾‾

3.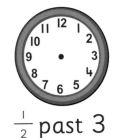
half past 5

4.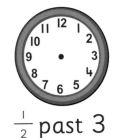
$\frac{1}{2}$ past 3

5. **Jess bought two lollipops for 23c each. How much did she spend altogether?**

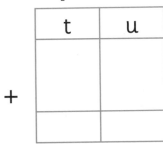

t	u

+

6. **A pencil costs 34c. Anna has 50c. How much change will she get?** ☐ c

7. **True or False ✓ or ✗**

    a) A mug holds more than 1 litre. ☐

    b) A banana is heavier than 1 kilogram. ☐

8. **Finish the pattern.**

2		6			14			20

5			25			40		

Curriculum Objective:
To revise concepts that were explored in units 31–39.